Arban's Complete Conservatory Method for TRUMPET

J. B. ARBAN

ALLEGRO EDITIONS

Copyright © 1912 J.B. Arban

Published by Allegro Editions

ISBN: 978-1-62654-039-2

Printed and bound in the United States of America

A LIST OF THE PRINCIPAL WORDS USED IN MODERN MUSIC.

WITH THEIR ABBREVIATIONS AND EXPLANATIONS.

A .... to, in, or at; *A tempo*, in time.
Accelerando (accel.) ..... Gradually increasing the speed.
Accent .... Emphasis on certain parts of the measure.
Adagio .... Slow; leisurely.
Ad libitum (ad lib.) .... At pleasure; not in strict time.
A due (a 2) .... To be played by both instruments.
Agitato .... Restless, with agitation.
Al or *Alla* .... In the style of.
Alla Marcia .... In the style of a March.
Allegretto .... Moderately quick.
Allegro .... Quick and lively.
Allegro assai .... Very rapidly.
Amore .... Love. *Con amore*, Fondly; tenderly.
Amoroso .... Affectionately.
Andante .... In moderately slow time.
Andantino .... A little less slow than Andante.
Anima, con } .... With animation.
Animato }
A piacere .... At pleasure.
Appassionato .... Impassioned.
Arpeggio .... A broken chord.
Assai .... Very: *Allegro assai*, very rapidly.
A tempo .... In the original movement.
Attacca .... Commence the next movement at once.
Barcarolle .... A Venetian boatman's song.
Ben .... Well; *Ben marcato*, well marked.
Bis .... Twice; repeat the passage.
Bravura .... Brilliant, bold, spirited.
Brillante .... Showy, sparkling, brilliant.
Brio, con .... With much spirit.
Cadenza .... A passage introduced as an embellishment.
Calando .... Decreasing in power and speed.
Cantabile .... In a singing style.
Caprice .... A composition of irregular construction.
Capriccio, a .... At pleasure.
Cavatina .... A movement in vocal style. [sounds.
Chord .... A combination of three or more musical
Coda .... A finishing movement.
Col or *con* .... With.
Crescendo (cres.) ... Gradually louder.
Da or *dal* .... From.
Da Capo (D. C.) ..... From the beginning.
Dal Segno (D. S.) ... From the sign.
Decrescendo (decresc.) . Decreasing in strength.
Delicatezza, con .... Delicately; refined in style.
Diminuendo (dim.) ... Gradually softer.
Divisi .... Divided. Each part to be played by a sepa-
Dolce .... Softly, sweetly. [rate instrument.
Dolcissimo .... Very sweetly and softly.
Dominant .... The fifth tone in the major or minor scale.
Duet or *duo* .... A composition for two performers.
E .... And.
Elegante .... Elegant; graceful.
Embouchure .... The mouthpiece of a wind instrument.
Enharmonic .... Alike in pitch but different in notation.
Energico .... With energy, vigorously.
Espressione, con .... Expressively, with expression.
Finale .... The concluding movement.
Fine .... The end.
Forte (f) .... Loud.
Forte-piano (fp) .... Loud and instantly soft again.
Fortissimo (ff) ..... Very loud.
Forza .... Force of tone.
Forzando (fz) .... Accentuate the sound.
Fuoco, con .... With fire; with spirit.
Furioso .... Furiously; passionately.
Giocoso .... Joyously; playfully.
Giusto .... Exact; in strict time.
Grandioso .... Grand; pompous; majestic.
Grave .... Very slow and solemn.
Grazioso .... Gracefully.
Gusto .... Taste.
Harmony .... A combination of musical sounds.
Key-note .... The first degree of the Scale.
Largamente .... Very broad in style.
Larghetto .... Slow, but not so slow as Largo.
Largo .... Broad and slow.
Legato .... Smoothly, the reverse of Staccato.
Leger-line .... A small added line above or below the staff.
Leggiero .... Lightly.
Lento .... Slow, but not as slow as Largo.
L'istesso tempo ..... In the same time.
Loco .... Play as written, no longer 8va.
Ma .... But. *Ma non troppo*, But not too much.
Maestoso .... Majestically, dignified.
Maggiore .... Major Key.
Marcato .... Marked. With distinctness and emphasis.

Meno .... Less. *Meno mosso*, Less quickly.
Mezzo .... Moderately.
Mezzo piano (mp) .... Moderately soft.
Mindre .... Minor Key.
Moderato .... Moderately. *Allegro moderato*, moderately
Molto .... Much; very. [fast.
Morendo .... Gradually softer.
Mosso .... Moved. *Piu mosso*, quicker.
Moto .... Motion. *Con moto*, with animation.
Non .... Not.
Notation .... { The art of representing musical sounds
                        { by characters visible to the eye.
Obligato .... An indispensable part.
Octave .... A series of 8 consecutive diatonic tones.
Opus (Op.) .... A work.
Ossia .... Or; or else. Generally indicating an easier
Ottava (8va) .... To be played an octave higher. [method.
Pause (⌢) .... The sign indicating pause or finish.
Perdendosi .... Dying away gradually.
Pesante .... Heavily; with firm and vigorous execution.
Piacere, a .... At pleasure.
Pianissimo (pp) ..... Very soft.
Piano (p) .... Soft.
Piu .... More. *Piu Allegro*, More quickly.
Poco or *un poco* ... A little.
Poco a poco .... Gradually, by degrees.
Poco piu mosso ...... A little faster.
Poco meno .... A little slower.
Poco piu .... A little faster.
Poi .... Then; afterwards.
Pomposo .... Pompous, grand.
Prestissimo .... As fast as possible.
Presto .... Very quick; faster than Allegro.
Primo (1mo) .... The first.
Quartet .... A piece of music for four performers.
Quasi .... As if; similar to; in the style of.
Quintet .... A piece of music for five performers.
Rallentando (rall.) . Gradually slower.
Rinforzando .... With special emphasis.
Ritardando (rit.) ... Slackening speed.
Risoluto .... Resolutely; bold; energetic.
Ritenuto .... Retarding the time.
Scherzando .... Playfully; sportively.
Secondo (2do) .... The second time (or part.)
Seconda volta .... The second time.
Segue .... Follow on in similar style.
Semplice .... Simply; unaffectedly.
Sempre .... Always; continually.
Senza .... Without. *Senza sordino*, Without mute.
Sforzando (sf) ...... Forcibly; with sudden emphasis.
Simile .... In like manner.
Smorzando (smorz.) .. Diminishing the sound.
Solo .... For one performer only.
Sordino .... A Mute. *Con Sordino*, With the Mute.
Sostenuto .... Sustained, prolonged.
Sotto .... Under. *Sotto voce*, In a subdued tone.
Spirito .... Spirit. *Con Spirito*, Forcefully.
Staccato .... Detached, separated.
Stentando .... Dragging or retarding the tempo.
Stretto .... An increase of speed. *Piu Stretto*, Faster.
Subdominant .... The 4th tone in the diatonic scale.
Syncopation .... Change of accent from a strong beat to a
Tacet .... Be silent. [weak one.
Tempo .... Movement.
Tempo primo .... As at first.
Tenuto (ten.) .... Held for the full value.
Theme .... The subject or melody.
Timbre .... Quality of tone.
Tonic .... The key-note of any scale.
Tremolo .... A trembling, fluttering movement.
Trio .... A piece of music for three performers.
Triplet .... { A group of 3 notes to be performed in the
                        { time of two of equal value.
Troppo .... Too much. *Allegro ma non troppo*, not too
Tutti .... All; all the instruments. [quick.
Un .... A; one; an.
Unison .... Alike in pitch.
Una corda .... On one string.
Variation .... The transformation and embellishment of a
Veloce .... Rapid; swift; quick. [melody.
Vibrato .... A wavy tone-effect which should be sparing-
Vivace .... With vivacity; bright; spirited. [ly used.
Vivo .... Lively.
Voce .... The voice; a certain part.
Volkslied .... A national or folk song.
Volti subito (V. S.) . Turn over quickly.

REPORT

of the Conservatory's Committee on Music Study regarding Mr. Arban's Cornet Method.

The Committee on Music Study has examined and tested the Method submitted to them by Mr. Arban.

This work is rich in instructive advice, is based upon the best of fundamental principles, and omits not a single instructive point which might be needed for the development and gradual technical perfection of a player.

The work might be classed as a general resumé of the ability and knowledge acquired by the author during his long experience as a teacher of and performer upon his instrument, and in a certain sense embodies the remarkable results achieved by him during his long career as a soloist.

Every variety of articulation, tonguing, staccati, etc., is thoroughly treated, ingeniously analyzed and clearly explained. The plentiful exercising material provided for each of these various difficulties is deserving of particular mention. Instructive points touching upon all possible musical questions are treated at length and throughout the work we have observed a profound appreciation of all difficulties and masterly ability to overcome them on the part of the author. The latter part of the work contains a long succession of studies, as interesting in subject as in form, and concludes with a collection of solos, which are, as it were, the embodiment or application of the previous lessons. These studies and solos give plentiful evidences of all those brilliant and thorough qualifications of which the author has so often given proof in his public performances.

In consequence the committee feels no hesitation in expressing its appreciation and approval of Mr. Arban's Method and recommends that same be adopted unreservedly for instruction at the Conservatory.

BERICHT

des Comités des Conservatoriums für musikalische Studien über die Cornet à Pistons-Schule des Herrn Arban.

Das Comité für musikalische Studien hat die Methode geprüft, welche ihm Herr Arban unterbreitet hat.

Dieses Werk enthält reichliche Aufklärungen, beruht auf ausgezeichneten Lehrsätzen und lässt keine Belehrungen bei Seite, die geeignet sind, einen guten Cornettisten zu bilden.

Es ist gewissermassen das Résumé der vom Verfasser erlangten Kenntnisse, die er in einer langen Praxis als Lehrer und ausübender Künstler gewonnen, und eine schriftliche Besiegelung der ausserordentlichen Resultate, die seine Carrière als Virtuos bezeichnen.

Die verschiedenen Arten der Articulation, des Zungenstosses, die Verzierungsnoten, die *Staccati*, sind gründlich abgehandelt, geistreich analysirt und glücklich gelöst. Die zahlreichen Lectionen, die ihnen der Autor widmet, haben ein Recht auf ganz besondere Erwähnung.

In der reichen Folge von Belehrungen, in denen auch alle sonstigen musikalischen Fragen behandelt sind, bemerkt man gleichzeitig eine ebenso tiefe Einsicht in die Schwierigkeiten als einen vollendeten Takt, ihrer Herr zu werden. Der letzte Theil des Werkes enthält eine lange Reihe von Etuden, ebenso interessant durch ihren Inhalt als durch ihre Form, und schliesst mit der Sammlung von Solostücken, die die practische Anwendung dessen, was vorher gelehrt wurde, enthalten. Aus diesen Etuden und Solos leuchten alle die glänzenden und soliden Eigenschaften hervor, von denen der Verfasser so oft Proben gegeben hat.

In Folge dessen steht das Comité nicht an, in gerechter Anerkennung des Verdienstes und der Nützlichkeit der Methode, deren Autor Herr Arban ist, dieselbe für den Unterricht im Conservatorium einzuführen.

RAPPORT

du Comité des Études musicales du Conservatoire, sur la Méthode de Cornet à pistons et de Saxhorn de M. Arban.

Le Comité des études musicales a examiné la Méthode qui lui a été soumise par M. Arban.

Cet ouvrage, comportant des développements considérables, repose sur d'excellentes doctrines et n'omet aucun des enseignements propres à former un bon cornettiste.

C'est, en quelque sorte, le résumé des connaissances acquises par l'auteur, au moyen d'une longue pratique comme professeur et exécutant, et une consécration écrite des résultats exceptionnels dont a été marquée sa carrière de virtuose.

Les différents genres d'articulations, les divers coups de langue, les notes d'agrément, les *staccati* sont sérieusement abordés, ingénieusement analysés et heureusement résolus; les nombreuses leçons qu'y consacre l'auteur ont droit à une mention toute particulière.

Dans la riche série d'enseignements où sont traitées toutes les autres question musicales, on remarque également une intelligence approfondie des difficultés et un tact parfait à en triompher. La dernière partie de l'ouvrage renferme une longue suite d'études aussi intéressantes par le fond que par la forme, et se termine par une collection de solos qui sont comme la mise en œuvre de ce qui a été enseigné précédemment: dans ces études et dans ces solos brillent les qualités éclatantes et solides à la fois dont l'auteur a si souvent fait preuve.

En conséquence, le Comité, rendant hommage au mérite et à l'utilité de la Méthode dont M. Arban est l'auteur, n'hésite pas à l'approuver, ainsi qu'à l'adopter pour l'enseignement au Conservatoire.

AUBER, MEYERBEER, KASTNER, A. THOMAS,
REBER, BAZIN, BENOIST, DAUVERNÉ, VOGT, PRUMIER, EMILE PERRIN,

EDOUARD MONNAIS, A. DE BEAUCHESNE,

Imperial Commissioner.   *Secretary.*

Biographical Sketch of Joseph-Jean-Baptiste-Laurent Arban.

This illustrious artist was born at Lyons, France, February 28, 1825. He entered the Conservatory at an early age, taking up the study of the trumpet under Dauverne, and won first prize in 1845. His military term was passed in the navy on board the "La Belle Poule," whose chief musician, Paulus became Chief Musician of the Garde à Paris during the reign of Napoleon III.

After having been professor of Saxhorn at the Military school (1857), he was elected professor of Cornet at the Conservatory January 23, 1869. After attending to these duties for a term of five years, Arban left the Conservatory for six years, returning again in 1880.

He was the most brilliant cornet player of his time, and his astonishing performances and triumphant concert tours throughout Europe were the means of establishing the Valve Cornet as one of the most popular of all musical instruments. Arban's artistic ideals, sound musicianship and invaluable instructive principles were perpetuated in his splendid "Method for the Cornet," which has succeeded in maintaining the very highest position among similar instructive works and which has never been surpassed in point of practical superiority or artistic plan.

Arban died at Paris on April 9, 1889. He was an officer of the Academie, Knight of the Order of Leopold of Belgium, of Christ of Portugal, and of Isabella the Catholic, and of the Cross of Russia.

Joseph-Jean-Baptiste-Laurent Arban.
Biographische Skizze.

Dieser berühmte Künstler sah in Lyons, Frankreich, am 28-ten Feb. 1825, das Licht der Welt. In jugendlichen Alter trat er in das Konservatorium ein, um unter Dauverne Unterricht auf der Trompete zu nehmen, und in Jahre 1845 gewann er den ersten Preis. Seine Dienstzeit absolvirte er bei der Marine an Bord der "La Belle Poule," deren Kapellmeister, Paulus, Kapellmeister der Garde à Paris wurde wärend der Regierung Napoleons III.

Nachdem er an der Militär Schule Lehrer für Saxhorn gewesen (1857), wurde er zum Cornet Lehrer gewählt am Konservatorium, am 23-ten Januar, 1869. Nachdem er sich dieser Thätigkeit fünf Jahre lang gewidmet hatte, verliess Arban das Konservatorium auf sechs Jahre, im Jahre 1880 dorthin zurück-kehrend.

Er war der hervorragendste Cornettist seiner Zeit, und seine erstaunliche Fertigkeit, sowie seine Triumphe auf allen Konzertbühnen Europas, machten das Cornet à Pistons bald zu einem der beliebtesten aller Musik Instrumente. Arban's künstlerisches Ideal, seine musikalische Tüchtigkeit und seine unvergleichlichen Lehrgrundsätze, wurden verewigt in seiner ausgezeichneten Cornet-Methode, welche noch immer den ersten Platz unter derartigen Werken für Lehrzwecke behauptet, und noch nie übertroffen worden ist, was praktischen Wert und künstlerische Anlage betrifft.

Arban starb in Paris am 9-ten April, 1889. Er war Mitglied der Akademie, Ritter des belgischen Leopold Ordens, des Christi von Portugal, des Katholischen Isabellen Ordens und des russischen Kreuzes.

Trait Biographique de la vie de Joseph-Jean-Baptiste-Laurent Arban.

Ce célébre musicien est né a Lyon, en France, le 28-me Fevrier, 1825. Il fut élève du Conservatoire encore jeune, pour étudier la trompette sous Daverné, et obtint le premier prix en 1845. Son devoir militaire fut passé dans la marine sur "La Belle Poule" donc le chef de musique, Paulus, devint chef de musique de la Garde à Paris pendant le reigne de Napoleon III.

Après avoir été professeur de la classe de saxhorn a l'école militaire (1857) il fut nommé professeur d'une classe de cornet au Conservatoire le 23-me Janvier, 1869. Après qu'il s'était devoué à ces devoirs pendant une période de cinque ans, Arban quitta le Conservatoire pour six ans, retournant de nouveau en 1880.

Il était le plus brillant cornettiste de son jour et son jeu étonnant, ainsi que les triomphes que lui accordait toute l'Europe pendant ses tournées de concerts, furent le moyen d'etablir le cornet à pistons comme un des plus populaires d'instruments musicals. Arban a perpetué son ideal d'Art, son profond savoir musical, et ses remarquables principes instructifs dans son excellente Methode pour le Cornet qui retient encore le premier rang parmi les oeuvres instructifs de méne genre, et n'a jamais été surpassée au point de superiorité pratique ou de plan artistique.

Arban mourut a Paris le 9-me Avril, 1889. Il était un officier de l'Académie, Chevalier de l'Ordre de Leopold de Belge, de Christ de Portugal, d'Isabelle la Catholique, et de la Croix Russe.

PREFACE.

It may appear somewhat strange to undertake the defense of the cornet at a time when this instrument has given proofs of its excellence, both in the orchestra and in solo performances, where it is no less indispensable to the composer, and not less liked by the public than the flute, the clarinet, and even the violin; where, in short, it has definitely won for itself the elevated position to which the beauty of its tone, the perfection of its mechanism and the immensity of its resources, so justly entitle it.

But this was not always the case; the cornet was far less successful when it first appeared; and, indeed, not many years ago, the masses treated the instrument with supreme indifference, while that time-honored antagonist — routine — contested its qualities, and strove hard to prohibit their application. This phenomenon, however, is of never-failing recurrence at the birth of every new invention, however excellent it may be, and of this fact the appearance of the saxhorn and the saxophone, instruments of still more recent date than the cornet, gave a new and striking proof.

The first musicians who played the cornet were, for the most part, either horn or trumpet players. Each imparted to his performance the peculiarities resulting from his tastes, his abilities and his habits, and I need scarcely add that the kind of execution which resulted from so many incomplete and heterogeneous elements was deficient in the extreme, and, for a long while, presented the lamentable spectacle of imperfections and failures of the most painful description.

Gradually, however, matters assumed a more favorable aspect. Executants, really worthy of the name of artists, began to make their appearance. However, regardless of the brilliant accomplishments of such performers, they could not deny the faults of their original training, viz., the total lack of qualifications necessary for ensemble playing, and decided musicianly tendencies. Some excited admiration for their extreme agility; others were applauded for the expression with which they played; one was remarkable for lip; another for the high tone to which he ascended; others for the brilliancy and volume of their tone. In my opinion, it was the reign of specialists, but it does not appear that a single one of the players then in vogue ever thought of realizing or of obtaining the sum total of qualities which alone can constitute a great artist.

This, then, is the point upon which I wish to insist, and to which I wish to call particular attention. At the present time, the incompleteness of the old school of performers is unanimously acknowledged, as is also the insufficiency of their instruction. That which is required is methodical execution and methodical instruction. It is not sufficient to phrase well or to execute difficult passages with skill. It is necessary that both these things should be equally well done.

VORREDE.

Es könnte sonderbar oder überflüssig erscheinen, heut zu Tage ein Wort zur Vertheidigung des Cornet à Pistons zu verlieren, wo dieses Instrument seine Proben im Orchester und Solo bestanden, wo es dem Componisten ebenso unentbehrlich und vom Publicum ebenso geschätzt ist, als die Flöte, die Clarinette und selbst die Violine, heut, wo es sich entschieden denjenigen Rang erobert hat, den ihm die Schönheit seines Klanges, die Vollendung seines Mechanismus und die Unermesslichkeit seiner Hülfsquellen anweisen.

Aber es ist nicht immer so gewesen. Das Cornet hat bescheidenere Anfänge gehabt, und es ist noch nicht viele Jahre her, dass man es allgemein mit stolzer Gleichgültigkeit aufnahm und zu gleicher Zeit die heilige Phalanx der Routine seine guten Eigenschaften bestritt und sich Mühe gab seine Anwendung zu proscribiren, eine Erscheinung, welche übrigens bei keiner neuen Erfindung sich zu zeigen verfehlt, mag diese auch noch so ausgezeichnet sein, und von der das Auftauchen des Saxhornes und Saxophons, jüngere Instrumente als das Cornet, neue und eclatante Beweise geliefert hat.

Die ersten Musiker, welche das Cornet à Pistons bliesen, waren in der Regel Hornisten oder Trompeter. Jeder that die Eigenthümlichkeit seines Geschmacks, seiner Fähigkeiten und Gewohnheiten hinzu, und ich brauche nicht zu bemerken, dass eine Execution, die aus so viel unvollkommenen und fremdartigen Elementen entstand, lange Zeit zu wünschen übrig liess, und ebenso lange das traurige Schauspiel der verletzendsten Lücken, Unvollkommenheiten und Fehler darbot.

Nach und nach änderten sich die Dinge zum Besseren. Man sah Bläser auftreten, die mit Recht Künstler genannt werden konnten. Wie glänzend indessen auch diese Individualitäten waren, so konnten sie doch die Fehler ihres Ursprungs nicht verleugnen, d. h. den vollständigen Mangel an Vielseitigkeit und bestimmter Leitung. Bei diesen bewunderte man den höchsten Grad der Fertigkeit, jene wurden wegen des Ausdrucks ihres Spiels applaudirt. Die Einen wurden wegen ihrer Lippenkraft gerühmt, andere wegen der Leichtigkeit ihrer Höhe, andere endlich wegen des Glanzes oder Volumens ihres Tones. Es herrschte, um mich so auszudrücken, das Reich der Specialitäten. Aber man sieht nicht, dass ein einziger der beliebten Cornettisten jener Epoche daran gedacht oder es sich vorgesetzt hätte, die Summe dieser Qualitäten zu erlangen, welche allein den wahren Künstler ausmachen.

Dies ist der Punkt, bei welchem ich verweilen und auf den ich besonders die Aufmerksamkeit hinlenken wollte. In unserer Zeit hat man einstimmig die Unzulänglichkeit der alten Virtuosen sowie ihrer Art des Unterrichtes anerkannt. Was man verlangt ist methodische Ausbildung. Es genügt nicht, die Gesangstellen gut zu blasen oder die

AVANT-PROPOS.

Il peut paraître étrange ou superflu de venir prendre la défense du cornet à pistons, aujourd'hui que cet instrument a fait ses preuves dans l'orchestre et dans le solo; qu'il n'est pas moins indispensable au compositeur ni moins aimé du public que la flûte, la clarinette, et même le violon: aujourd'hui enfin qu'il a définitivement conquis le rang élevé que lui assignent la beauté de son timbre, la perfection de son mécanisme et l'immensité de ses ressources.

Mais il n'en a pas été toujours ainsi: le cornet a eu des commencements plus modestes, et il n'y a pas encore beaucoup d'années que les masses l'accueillaient avec une superbe indifférence, en même temps que le bataillon sacré de la routine contestait ses qualités, et s'efforçait d'en proscrire l'application, phénomène qui, d'ailleurs, ne manque jamais de se produire, à l'origine de toute invention nouvelle, si excellente soit-elle, et dont l'apparition du saxhorn et du saxophone, instruments plus jeunes que le cornet, a fourni une éclatante et nouvelle preuve.

Les premiers musiciens qui jouèrent du cornet à pistons furent en général des cornistes et des trompettistes. Chacun y apporta le cachet de ses goûts, de ses facultés, de ses habitudes, et je n'ai pas besoin d'ajouter qu'une exécution née d'éléments incomplets autant qu'hétérogènes, laissa bien longtemps à désirer, et offrit pendant une période assez prolongée le triste spectacle des lacunes, des défaillances et des défauts les plus choquants.

Peu à peu les choses se modifièrent dans un sens favorable; l'on vit surgir des exécutants véritablement dignes du nom d'artistes. Cependant, quelque brillantes que fussent ces individualités, elles ne purent se soustraire au vice de leur origine, c'est à-dire au manque absolu d'ensemble et de direction. Chez ceux-ci on admira une agilité extrême, ceux-là se firent applaudir par l'expression de leur jeu; les uns furent cités pour leurs lèvres, les autres pour leur facilité à monter, d'autres enfin, pour l'éclat ou le volume de leur son: ce fut, si je puis parler ainsi, le règne de spécialités; mais on ne voit pas qu'un seul des cornettistes en vogue à cette époque, ait songé à réaliser ou se soit proposé d'acquérir la somme des qualités qui seules constituent les grands artistes.

C'est là le point sur lequel je voulais insister et particulièrement appeler l'attention. De nos jours, on a unanimement reconnu l'insuffisance des anciens virtuoses, comme aussi l'insuffisance de leur enseignement. Ce que l'on veut, c'est une exécution, c'est un enseignement méthodique; il ne suffit pas de bien chanter ou de bien faire la difficulté, il faut faire égale-

— IV —

In a word, it is necessary that the cornet, as well as the flute, the clarinet, the violin, and the voice, should possess the pure style and the grand method of which a few professors, the Conservatory in particular, have conserved the precious secret and the salutary traditions.

This is the aim which I have incessantly kept in view throughout my long career; and if a numerous series of brilliant successes (obtained in the presence of the most competent judges and the most critical audiences),* give me the right to believe that I have, at any rate, approached the desired end, I shall not be laying myself open to the charge of presumption, in confidently entering upon the delicate mission of transmitting to others the results of my own thorough studies and assiduous practice. I have long been a professor, and this work is to a certain extent, merely the resumé of a long experience, which each day has brought nearer to perfection.

My explanations will be found as short and clear as possible, for I wish to instruct and not to terrify the student. Long pages of "text" are not always read, and it is highly advantageous to replace the latter by exercises and examples. This is the wealth which I consider cannot be too lavishly accumulated; this is the source which can never be too plentifully drawn from. This, however, will be perceived from the extent of the present volume, in which, in my opinion, will be found the solution of all difficulties and of all problems.

I have endeavored throughout to compose studies of a melodic nature, and in general to render the study of the instrument as agreeable as possible. In a word, I have endeavored to lead the pupil, without discouragement, to the highest limits of execution, sentiment and style, destined to characterize the new school.

J. B. ARBAN.

---

*) The results which I have obtained in France, Germany and England victoriously plead the cause of the cornet and prove that the latter can compete with the most popular of instruments. In a concert given by the "Societé des Concerts du Conservatoire" in 1848, I played the famous air for the flute composed by Boehm on a Swiss theme, comprising, as is well known, an intentional combination of enormous difficulties. From that day forth I may say the cornet took its place among classic instruments. In the piece of music just alluded to, I performed the flute tonguing in double staccato, also the triple staccato, which I am the first to have applied to the cornet.

Schwierigkeiten leicht zu überwinden, man soll das Eine ebenso wie das Andere können; mit einem Wort, es muss für das Cornet à Pistons ebenso, wie für die Flöte, die Clarinette, die Violine und die Stimme, jener schöne Styl und jene grosse Schule geschaffen werden, deren kostbaren Schatz und deren heilsame Traditionen gewisse Professoren, und namentlich das Conservatoire bewahren.

Dies ist das Ziel, welches ich in meiner schon ziemlich langen Carrière niemals zu verfolgen aufgehört habe, und wenn zahlreiche und eclatante Erfolge vor den competentesten Richtern wie vor den difficilsten Zuhörern*) mich zu glauben berechtigen, dass ich ihm ziemlich nahe gekommen bin, so wird es nicht als Dünkel erscheinen, wenn ich mit Selbstvertrauen die bedenkliche Mission verfolge, auch auf Andere die Früchte der gründlichsten Studien und der fleissigsten Uebung zu übertragen. Uebrigens lehre ich schon eine ziemlich geraume Zeit und dieses Buch ist gewissermassen nur das Résumé einer langjährigen nnd täglich vervollkommneten Erfahrung.

Meine Erklärungen werden so kurz und deutlich als möglich sein, denn ich will den Schüler belehren und nicht erschrecken. Man liest nicht immer lange Seiten Text und es ist vortheilhafter, statt dessen Uebungen und Beispiele zu geben. Dies sind die Reichthümer, die ich nie zu sehr anhäufen, die Quellen, aus denen ich nie zu reichlich schöpfen zu können glaubte, und zwar zum Vortheil dieses Buches, denn man sollte, nach meinem Sinne, darin die Lösung aller Schwierigkeiten und aller Probleme finden.

Ich habe mich beständig befleissigt, melodische Etuden zu componiren und überhaupt gesucht, das Studium des Instrumentes so angenehm wie möglich zu machen, mit einem Wort: den Schüler, ohne ihn zu entmuthigen, bis zu den äussersten Grenzen der Fertigkeit, des Ausdrucks und des Styls zu führen, soll das Wesen dieser neuen Schule sein.

J. B. ARBAN.

---

*) Die Erfolge, welche ich in Frankreich, Deutschland und England gehabt, sprechen siegreich für die Sache des Cornet à Pistons und beweisen, dass dieses den beliebtesten Instrumenten den Rang streitig machen kann. Im Jahre 1848 liess ich mich in einem Concerte des Conservatoriums hören, wo ich die berühmte Arie für die Flöte, comp von Böhm über ein schweizer Thema, spielte, und in welcher, wie man weiss, die ausgesuchtesten Schwierigkeiten enthalten sind. Von diesem Tage, kann ich sagen, datirt es, dass das Cornet à Pistons seine Stelle unter den classischen Instrumenten eingenommen hat. Es war in diesem Stücke, wo ich den Zungenstoss der Flöte im zweiten Staccato hören liess, und ebenso das dreifache Staccato, dessen Anwendung auf dem Cornet à Pistons von mir zuerst geschehen ist.

---

ment bien l'un et l'autre; en un mot, il faut que le cornet à pistons, de même que la flûte, la clarinette, le violon et la voix, ait ce beau style et cette grande école dont quelques professeurs, et en particulier le Conservatoire, ont conservé le précieux dépôt et les saines traditions.

Tel est le but que je n'ai cessé de poursuivre dans ma carrière déjà longue; et si de nombreux, d'éclatants succès, devant les juges les plus compétents comme devant les auditeurs les plus difficiles*), me donnent le droit de croire que j'en ai approché d'assez près, je ne montrerai pas de présomption, en abordant avec confiance la mission délicate de transmettre à d'autres le fruit de l'étude la plus approfondie et de la pratique la plus assidue. Il y a déjà d'ailleurs bien longtemps que je professe, et ce livre n'est en quelque sorte que le résumé d'une expérience longuement acquise et chaque jour perfectionée.

Mes explications seront aussi brèves et aussi claires que possible, car je veux instruire l'élève, et non pas l'effrayer. On ne lit pas toujours les longues pages de texte, et il y a tout profit à les remplacer par des exercises et des exemples. Voilà les richesses que j'ai cru ne jamais pouvoir trop accumuler, les sources auxquelles j'ai cru ne pouvoir jamais puiser d'une main trop large, comme on s'en apercevra, du reste, à l'importance de ce volume, car on y doit trouver, à mon sens, la solution de toutes les difficultés et de tous les problèmes.

Je me suis constamment appliqué à composer des études mélodiques, et généralement à rendre l'étude de l'instrument aussi agréable que possible; en un mot, à conduire sans qu'il se décourage, l'élève jusqu'aux dernières limites de l'exécution, du sentiment et du style qui doivent caractériser la nouvelle école.

J. B. ARBAN.

---

*) Les résultats que j'ai obtenus en France, en Allemagne et en Angleterre, plaident victorieusement la cause du cornet à pistons et démontrent que celui-ci peut le disputer aux instruments les plus aimés. En 1848, je me fis entendre à une séance de la Société des Concerts du Conservatoire, où je jouai le fameux air de flûte composé par Boehm sur un thème suisse, et dans lequel sont, comme on sait, entassées à plaisir les plus inextriccables difficultés; à partir de ce jour, je puis dire que le cornet à pistons prit place à côté des instruments classiques. C'est dans ce morceau que je fis entendre le coup de langue de flûte en staccato binaire, ainsi que le staccato ternaire, dont je suis le premier à avoir fait l'application au cornet à pistons,

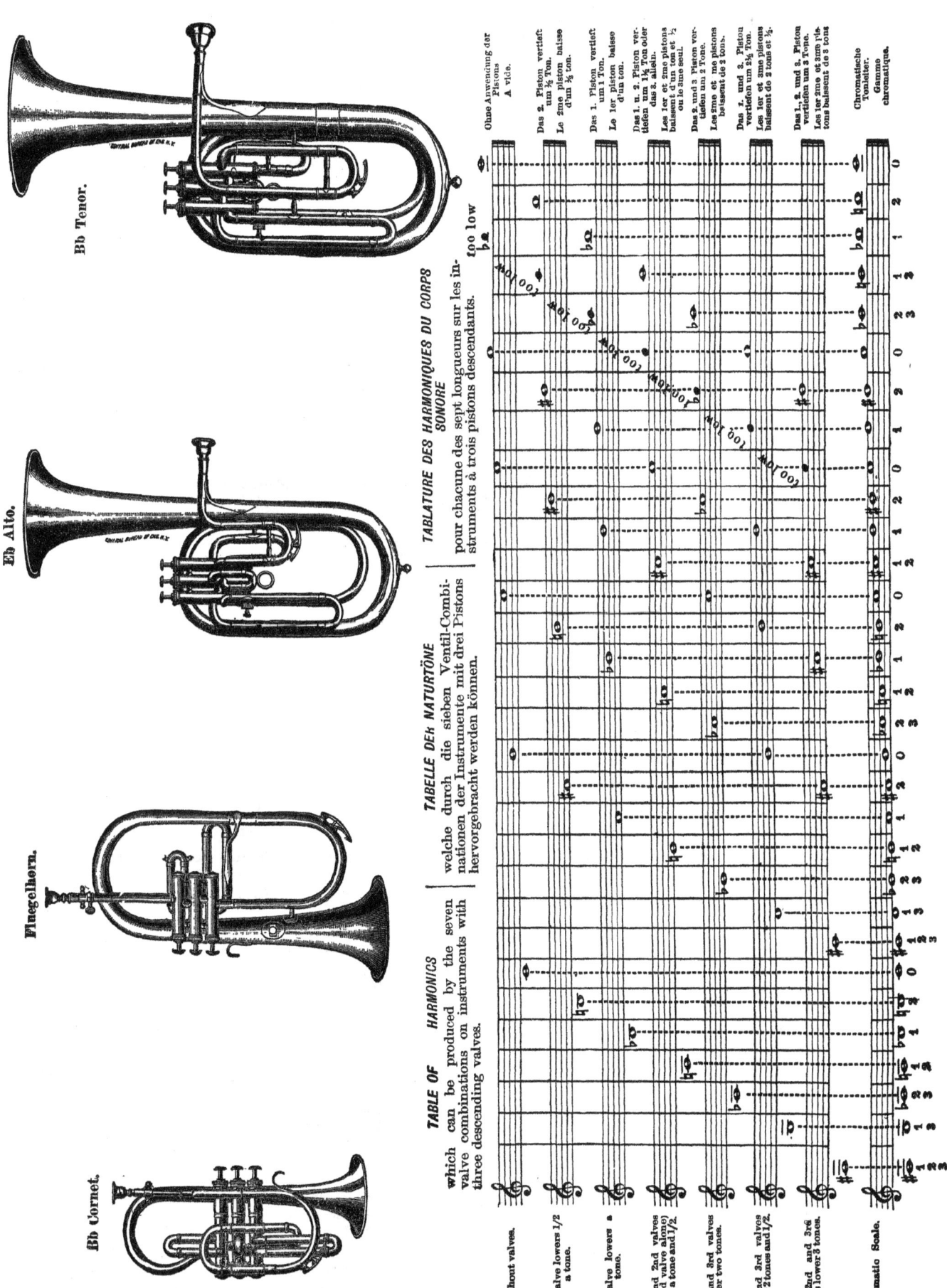

DIAGRAM OF CORNET
Giving Proper Names to the Various Parts of the Instrument

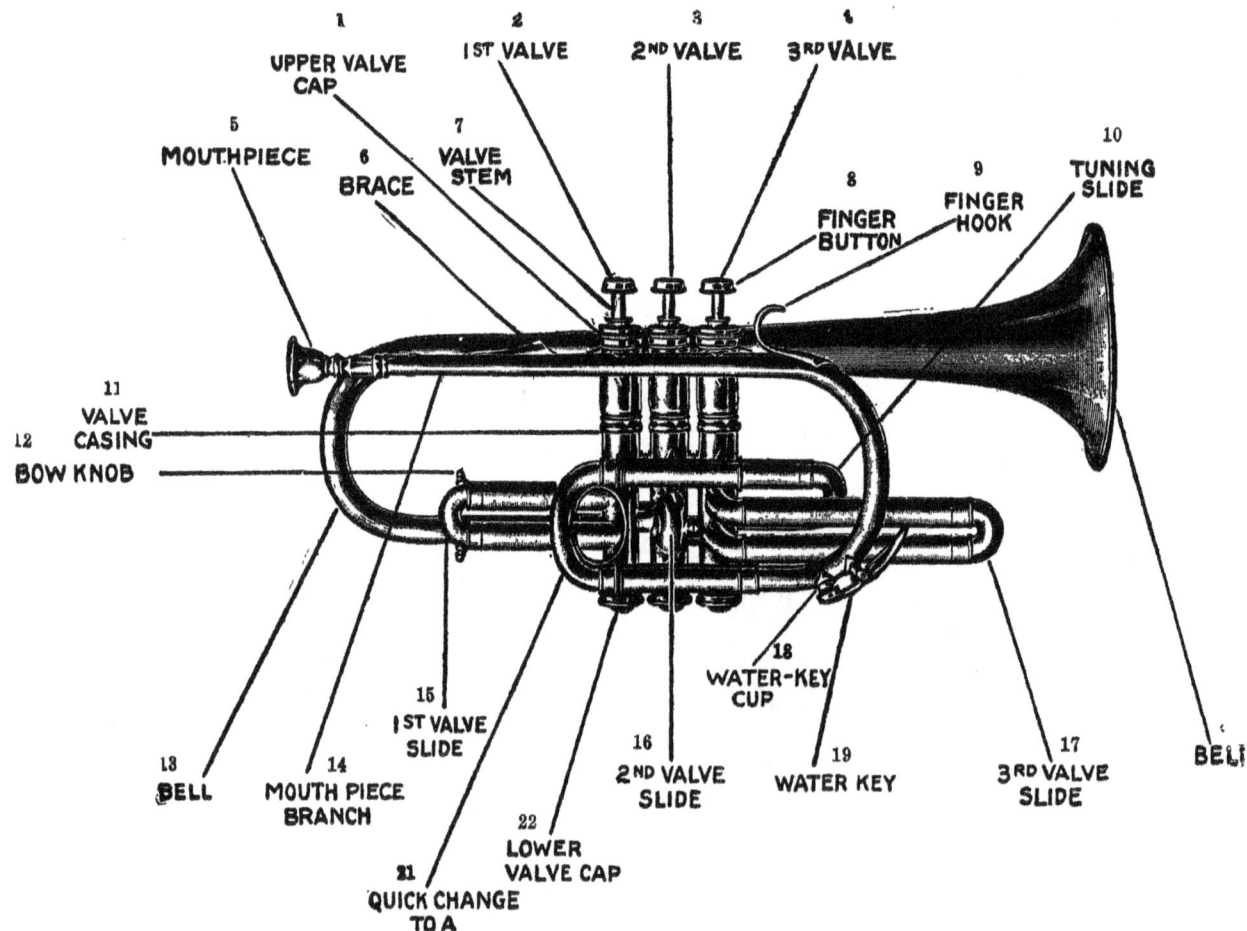

1. UPPER VALVE CAP
2. 1ST VALVE
3. 2ND VALVE
4. 3RD VALVE
5. MOUTHPIECE
6. BRACE
7. VALVE STEM
8. FINGER BUTTON
9. FINGER HOOK
10. TUNING SLIDE
11. VALVE CASING
12. BOW KNOB
13. BELL
14. MOUTH PIECE BRANCH
15. 1ST VALVE SLIDE
16. 2ND VALVE SLIDE
17. 3RD VALVE SLIDE
18. WATER-KEY CUP
19. WATER KEY
20. BELL
21. QUICK CHANGE TO A
22. LOWER VALVE CAP

The Cornet pictured above is a Besson New Creation (Long Model)

ABBILDUNG EINES CORNETS
Mit richtiger Bezeichnung der verschiedenen Teile des Instruments

1. Oberer Ventilschraubendeckel
2. 1-stes Ventil
3. 2-tes Ventil
4. 3-tes Ventil
5. Mundstück
6. Stütze
7. Ventilstange
8. Fingerknopf
9. Fingerhaken
10. Stimmzug
11. Aeusere Ventilhülse
12. Bogenknöpfchen
13. Schallbecherbogen
14. Mundstückröhre
15. 1-ster Ventilzug
16. 2-ter Ventilzug
17. 3-ter Ventilzug
18. Wasserklappenhülse
19. Wasserklappe
20. Schallbecher
21. Schnell-Wechsel Bogen für A Stimmung
22. Unterer Ventilschraubendeckel

DAS OBEN ABGEBILDETE CORNET IST EIN BESSON NEUER STYL (Langes Model)

ILLUSTRATION D'UM CORNET
Avec propre appelation des diverse parties du cornet

1. Chapeau du piston
2. 1-er piston
3. 2-me piston
4. 3-me piston
5. Embouchure du Cornet à piston
6. Traverse pour Soliditèr
7. Branche du piston
8. Boutons des pistons
9. Support du Cornet pour le petit doigt
10. Coulisse d'accord
11. Le tube des pistons ou Magasin
12. Support de la Coulisse
13. Grand tube ou pavillion
14. Coulisse de l'embouchure
15. 1-er coulisse
16. 2-me coulisse
17. 3-me coulisse
18. Bassin de la clef d'eau
19. Clef d'eau
20. Pavillon
21. Transpositeur de Sib en la
22. Cuvettes des pistons

CORNET ICI ILLUSTRÉ EST UN BESSON NOUVEAU STYL (MODEL ELONGÉ)

Compass of the Cornet.

As indicated in the accompanying table, the instruments with three valves have a chromatic range of two octaves and a half, which, in the case of the cornet and the alto, extends from F sharp below to C above the staff; however, not every player succeeds in mastering the whole of this range with clearness and facility. Therefore, when writing for these instruments, even if it is for a solo, it will be advisable not to use the extreme limits of the scale indicated in the foregoing table. As a rule, the higher registers of the instruments are employed much too frequently by arrangers and composers, in consequence of which the performer is apt to lose the beautiful and characteristic tonal qualities peculiar to his instrument. It also leads to failure to produce the simplest passages, even when called for in the middle register. To avoid this evil, it is necessary to continually practice the instrument throughout its entire register, and to pay special attention to the chapter devoted to the study of the various intervals.

The easiest portion of the cornet's range commences at low C and terminates at G above the staff. One may easily ascend as high as B flat, but the B natural and the C ought to be made use of very sparingly.

In regard to the notes below C:

Umfang des Cornet à pistons und des Flügelhorn.

Wie beiliegende Tafel angiebt, so haben die Instrumente mit drei absteigenden Pistons oder Ventilen einen chromatischen Umfang von 2½ Octaven, welcher sowohl bei dem Cornet, wie bei dem Flügelhorn vom Fis unter den Linien bis zum hohen C über den Linien reicht; indessen ist es nicht Jedem gegeben, diesen ganzen Umfang mit Leichtigkeit zu bewältigen.

Man muss also, wenn man für diese Instrumente schreibt, selbst bei einem Solo nicht bis zu den äussersten Grenzen der Tonleiter, welche auf der Tabelle angezeigt ist, schreiten. Im Allgemeinen führen die Herren Musikmeister die Instrumente in zu hohe Regionen; die Folge davon ist, dass der Künstler den schönen Ton seines Instrumentes verliert und ihm schliesslich die einfachsten Dinge versagen, selbst wenn er sich in den Mitteltönen bewegt. Um diesem Uebelstande vorzubeugen, ist es gut, das Instrument in seinem ganzen Umfange mit Beharrlichkeit zu üben, und besonders bei dem Kapitel zu verweilen, welches dem Studium der verschiedenen Intervalle gewidmet ist.

Der Umfang, welcher am leichtesten zu durchlaufen ist, geht vom C unter den Linien bis zum G über den Linien. Man kann ziemlich leicht bis zum B hinaufgehen, aber das H und C dürfen nur sehr selten angewendet werden.

Was die Töne betrifft, welche unterhalb des C liegen, also

Étendue du cornet à pistons et du saxhorn.

Ainsi que l'indique la tablature, les instruments à trois pistons descendants ont une étendue chromatique de deux octaves et ½, qui, pour le cornet aussi bien que pour le saxhorn, va du *fa* dièse au-dessous des lignes, jusqu'au contre *ut* au-dessus des lignes. Mais il n'est pas donné à tout le monde de parcourir avec facilité cette étendue toute entière.

Il faut donc, quand on écrit pour ces instruments, fût-ce même un solo, ne pas atteindre aux dernières limites de l'échelle indiquée sur la tablature. Généralement MM. les chefs de musique font monter les instruments dans les régions trop élevées. Il en résulte que l'artiste perd la belle qualité de son de l'instrument et qu'il finit par manquer les choses les plus simples, même quand il joue dans le médium. Pour obvier à cet inconvénient, il convient de travailler avec constance l'instrument dans toute son étendue et de s'appesantir plus particulièrement sur le chapitre consacré à l'étude des divers intervalles.

L'étendue la plus facile à parcourir commence à l'*ut* grave pour continuer jusqu'au *sol* au-dessus des lignes. On peut assez facilement monter jusqu'au *si* bémol, mais le *si* naturel et l'*ut* ne doivent s'employer que très-rarement.

Quant aux notes qui existent au-dessous de l'*ut* c'est-à-dire.

same do not present any very great difficulties, although some players experience considerable trouble in producing them with clearness and sonority. However, when properly produced, they are very beautiful and effective.

so bieten sie keine grossen Schwierigkeiten obschon gewisse Künstler zuweilen viel Mühe haben, sie mit Fülle hervorzubringen; diese Töne sind sehr schön, wenn man sie sich gut angeeignet hat.

elles n'offrent pas de grandes difficultés, bien que certains artistes éprouvent parfois beaucoup de peine à les faire sortir avec plénitude; ces notes sont cependant fort belles quand on les possède bien.

Cornet in C

It is indispensably necessary that the performer should play the cornets in C and B natural, as well as the one in B flat, as they may prove of great service in orchestra, especially for the performance of trumpet parts.

The cornet in C is a most brilliant solo instrument, its timbre, in some respects, being more preferable than that of the cornet in B flat. In theatres devoted to the performance of lyric works it is really indispensable on account of the ease and surety with which the highest intervals can be produced, and also on account of transpositions which are much easier on this than on the B flat cornet. If an orchestra number is written in the key of B natural, or in E major, it is advisable to play on a cornet pitched in B natural. If written in C or F the cornet in C should be employed. As for the cornet in A, it accords but poorly with any of the keys I have just been indicating, and its use would only serve to create unnecessary difficulties.*

*) Since the above was written, the cornet, together with every other wind instrument, has been brought to such a high state of perfection, as to do away entirely with many of the drawbacks of the old system. Nowadays the cornet in C is used to some slight extent by amateurs who desire to play from vocal music and who through use of this instrument avoid the necessity of transposition. It is seldom used by professionals. The cornet in A natural is entirely obsolete.
—*The Editor.*

Cornet à Pistons in C.

Es ist unerlässlich, die Cornets à pistons in C und H ebenso gut zu blasen, als das Cornet in B, denn sie können in dem Orchester grosse Dienste leisten, besonders wenn man dazu berufen ist, Trompetenstimmen auszuführen. Als Soloinstrument gehört das Cornet in C zu den brillantesten, und besitzt sogar ein edleres Timbre, als das in B. In den Theatern, die der Aufführung lyrischer Werke gewidmet sind, würde man nicht darauf verzichten können, wegen der Transpositionen, welche darauf viel leichter sind, als auf dem B-Cornet, und besonders wegen der Sicherheit, mit welcher man die höchsten Töne hervorbringen kann.

Wenn das Orchester in H-dur oder E-dur spielt, ist es gut, auf dem Cornet in H zu blasen. Wenn das Orchester in C oder F spielt, muss man das Cornet in C nehmen. Was das Cornet in A betrifft, so correspondirt es sehr schlecht mit den Tonarten, welche ich für das Orchester angegeben habe, und seine Anwendung würde im Allgemeinen nur Schwierigkeiten verursachen.*

*) Seitdem Obiges geschrieben wurde, ist das Cornet, wie alle anderen Blas-instrumente, bis zu so hochgradiger Vollkommenheit gebracht worden, das viele Nachteile des alten Systems gänzlich beseitigt worden und heutzutage wird das C-Cornet nur hier und da von Dillettanten gebraucht welche nach Noten für Singstimme spielen wollen und durch den Gebrauch dieses Instruments vermeiden sie die sonst notwendige Transposition. Es wird selten von Berufsmusikern gebraucht. Das H-Cornet ist vollständig veraltet.
—*Der Herausgeber.*

Cornet à pistons en ut.

Il est indispensable de jouer le cornet à pistons en *ut* et en *si* naturel aussi bien que le cornet en *si* bémol, car ils peuvent rendre de très-grands services dans les orchestres, surtout quand on est appelé à jouer des parties de trompettes. Comme instrument solo, le cornet en *ut* est des plus brillants et possède même un timbre plus distingué que celui en *si* bémol. Dans les théâtres consacrés aux représentations lyriques, on ne saurait s'en passer, à cause des transpositions qui y deviennent beaucoup plus faciles que sur le cornet à pistons en *si* bémol, et surtout en raison de la sûreté avec laquelle on peut atteindre les sons les plus aigus.

Si l'orchestre joue en *si* naturel ou en *mi* majeur, il convient de jouer avec le cornet en *si* naturel. Si l'orchestre joue en *ut* ou en *fa*, alors prenez le cornet en *ut*. Quant au cornet en *la*, il correspond assez mal aux tons que je viens d'indiquer pour l'orchestre et son emploi ne ferait, en général, que créer des difficultés.*

*) Depuis que le sus-dit fut ecrit, le cornet a pistons, comme touts autres instruments à vent a été perfectionné de telle manière que beaucoup de désavantages du vieil système ont été éliminés. Aujourdhui un certain nombre d'amateurs se servent du Do-Cornet quand ils veulent jouer de la musique a chant et en usant cet instrument, ils évident la transposition qui autrement aurait été nécessaire. Les professionels ne s'en servent que bien rarement. Le Si-Cornet est complètement tombe en désuétude.
—*l'Editeur.*

Second Table.

Suggestions are offered herewith for producing F natural below the staff and at the same time for facilitating certain passages, which, with the fingering indicated in the first table, are well-nigh impossible. In order to achieve this, the slide of the third valve should be drawn out one-half tone, in order to obtain a length of two tones, instead of the usual one and one-half tones. In doing this, it will be advisable to adopt the following fingering, which is very popular among German Cavalry trumpeters.

Zweite Tabelle.

Es giebt ein Mittel, das F unter den Linien zu erhalten, und zugleich die Ausführung gewisser Passagen zu erleichtern, welche mit dem in der ersten Tabelle angegebenen Fingersatze unausführbar sind. Zu diesem Zwecke muss man den Zugbogen des dritten Pistons um einen halben Ton herausziehen, um so eine Länge von zwei Tönen zu erhalten anstatt der gewöhnlichen von 1½ Ton. Man wird sich dann des folgenden Fingersatzes bedienen, der übrigens in Deutschland bei Cavallerie-Musik sehr gebräuchlich ist.

Deuxième Tablature.

Il existe un moyen d'obtenir le *fa* naturel au-dessous des lignes, et en même temps de faciliter l'exécution de certains passages impraticables avec les doigtés indiqués sur la première tablature. Il faut, pour cela, tirer d'un demi-ton la coulisse du troisième piston, de manière à réaliser une longueur de deux tons, au lieu d'un ton et demi qu'elle possède habituellement. On se servira alors du doigté suivant qui, d'ailleurs, est fort usité en Allemagne.

In order that the F natural may be produced in perfect tune, the tuning slide should be drawn out a little. (I shall explain this more fully in the next chapter.)
Example of trills impossible with the ordinary fingering, but quite easy with the fingering as shown in this second table.

Man muss, damit das F vollständig rein wird, zu gleicher Zeit den Stimmbogen ein wenig herausziehen, wie ich in dem nächsten Capitel mittheilen werde.
Beispiel der mit dem gewöhnlichen Fingersatz unausführbaren Triller, die man aber leicht bei Anwendung des Fingersatzes der zweiten Tabelle hervorbringen kann:

Il faut, pour que le *fa* naturel soit tout à fait juste, tirer en même temps un peu la coulisse d'accord, ainsi que je l'indiquerai dans le prochain chapitre.
Exemple de trilles impraticables avec le doigté ordinaire, et que l'on peut obtenir facilement en employant le doigté de la deuxième tablature:

Examples of special passages, showing how forked fingering may be avoided:

Beispiel einiger Figuren, in welchen man bei Anwendung desselben Fingersatzes die Gabeln vermeiden kann:

Exemples de quelques traits dans lesquels on peut éviter les fourches en employant ce même doigté:

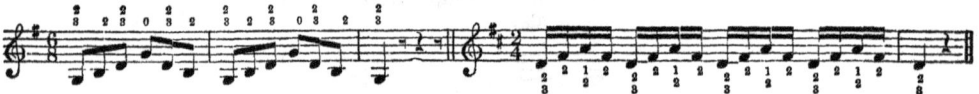

Only in exceptional cases should expedients such as the above be employed. I have only called attention to them here in order to acquaint the student with all the resources of the instrument.

Man darf nur in Ausnahmefällen zu diesem Verfahren seine Zuflucht nehmen; ich gebe es hier nur, um mit allen Hülfsmitteln des Instrumentes bekannt zu machen.

On ne doit recourir à ces procédés que dans des cas exceptionnels; je ne les donne ici que pour faire bien connaître toutes les ressources de l'instrument.

Use of the Tuning Slide

A well-constructed cornet ought to be so mounted that the thumb of the left hand should be able to enter the ring of the tuning slide, and open and shut it at pleasure, without the help of the right hand. It is then possible to regulate the pitch of the instrument while playing. It is generally known that when beginning to play with a cold instrument the latter will always be a little below pitch. After a few measures have been played, and the instrument is warmed, it will sharpen very rapidly.

The slide is also used for the purpose of equalizing all those notes which, in the course of natural production, are rendered too high. Each valve is tuned for separate use, and the natural consequence is that when several are employed simultaneously the slides get too short and the precision of tone is inevitably affected. Here is a practical example: Let us suppose that the player will use a G crook on a B flat cornet; this will lower the instrument one tone and a half. In order to play in tune in this new key it will be necessary to draw out the slide of each valve considerably.

*) In the estimation of acknowledged modern authorities on cornet playing, there is no necessity for playing the F below the staff, as it is really not within the legitimate range of the instrument.—*The Editor.*

Anwendung des Stimmbogens.

Ein gut gearbeitetes Cornet à pistons soll so beschaffen sein, dass der Daumen der linken Hand in den Ring des Stimmbogens hineingehen kann, um ihn ohne Hülfe der rechten Hand nach Belieben zu öffnen und zu schliessen. Man kann also während des Blasens stimmen. Jedermann weiss, dass wenn man anfängt zu spielen, das Instrument, da es kalt ist, ein wenig zu tief steht. Erst nach der Ausführung einiger Takte steigt das Instrument, indem es warm wird, und zwar in einem ausserordentlichen Verhältniss.

Der Stimmbogen soll dazu dienen, die Töne, welche von Natur zu hoch sind, auszugleichen. Da jedes Piston abgestimmt ist, um es einzeln anzuwenden, so werden, wenn man mehrere zusammenfügt, die Zugbogen zu kurz und die Genauigkeit leidet darunter. Hier ein Beispiel: Gesetzt, man brächte auf das Cornet à pistons in B ein Versatzstück, und dieses wäre der Ton G, so steht das Instrument 1½ Ton tiefer. Um in der neuen Stimmung richtig zu blasen, ist es nothwendig, den Bogen eines jeden Pistons bedeutend auszuziehen.

Emploi de la coulisse d'accord.

Un cornet à pistons bien fabriqué doit être monté de manière à ce que le pouce de la main gauche puisse entrer dans l'anneau de la coulisse d'accord, afin de pouvoir l'ouvrir et la fermer à volonté sans le secours de la main droite. On peut ainsi s'accorder en jouant; personne n'ignore que lorsqu'on commence à jouer, l'instrument, étant froid, se trouve un peu trop bas. Ce n'est qu'après l'exécution de quelques mesures que l'instrument monte en s'échauffant, et cela dans des proportions extraordinaires.

La coulisse d'accord doit servir aussi à compenser les notes qui, par leur nature, sont trop hautes. Chaque piston étant accordé pour être employé séparément, quand on en additionne plusieurs, les coulisses deviennent forcément trop courtes, et la justesse se trouve altérée. En voici un exemple: Supposez que sur le cornet à pistons en *si* bémol vous mettiez un corps de rechange, et que ce soit le ton de *sol*, l'instrument se trouve alors baissé d'un ton et demi. Pour jouer juste avec ce nouveau ton, il faut nécessairement tirer beaucoup la coulisse de chaque piston.

A similar effect is produced whenever the third valve is employed. For instance, when the third valve is pressed down on a B flat cornet, the latter is lowered one tone and a half; the effect is exactly as though the instrument were pitched in G, as the slides of each valve produce the effect of tones added to the instrument.

In such a case it would be necessary to draw the slides of the first and second valves in order to use them simultaneously with the third. But as such a proceeding is most impractical, it will be advisable to employ the above-mentioned device; that is, compensate for the want of length of the tubes by drawing the slide with the thumb of the left hand. Without this precaution every one of the following notes would be too high.

Eine gleiche Wirkung zeigt sich allemal, wenn man auf irgend einem Instrument das dritte Piston in Anwendung bringt. Wenn man auf dem *B*-Cornet das dritte Piston tiefer stellt, so macht man dasselbe um 1½ Ton tiefer; das ist gerade so, als ob man ein Instrument in *G* hat, da die Zugbogen eines jeden Pistons die Wirkung der Töne hervorbringen, welche dem Instrument durch Versatzstücke hinzugefügt sind.

In diesem Falle würde man die Bogen des ersten und zweiten Pistons herausziehen müssen, um sich ihrer in Gemeinschaft mit dem dritten bedienen zu können. Da aber diese Operation nicht gut thunlich ist, so wird es nothwendig, sich durch das oben angeführte Kunststück zu helfen, das heisst, was den Röhren an Länge gebricht, dadurch auszugleichen, dass man mit dem Daumen der linken Hand den Stimmbogen herauszieht; ohne diese Vorsichtsmaassregel würden alle Töne zu hoch werden.

Un effet analogue se produit toutes les fois que sur un instrument quelconque vous employez le troisième piston. Ainsi, lorsque sur un cornet en *si* bémol vous abaissez le troisième piston, vous le baissez d'un ton et demi: c'est exactement comme si vous aviez mis votre instrument en *sol*, puisque les coulisses de chaque piston produisent l'effet de tons ajoutés à l'instrument.

Il faudrait donc, dans ce cas, tirer les coulisses du premier et du deuxième piston, pour s'en servir collectivement avec le troisième; mais comme cette opération est impracticable, il devient nécessaire d'y suppléer l'artifice indiqué ci-dessous, c'est-à-dire de compenser le manque de longueur des tubes, en tirant la coulisse d'accord avec le pouce de la main gauche; sans cette précaution, toutes les notes ci-après seraient trop hautes.

It is not difficult to lower these notes through action of the lips, although the quality of the tone will invariably suffer through such a proceeding. Therefore, in order to insure proper tonal brilliancy, it is always better in slow movements to employ the slide as a compensatory medium.

Es ist nicht schwer, diese Töne vermittelst der Lippen herabzustimmen, aber dies geschieht auf Kosten der Güte des Tons. Es ist also besser in langsamen Tempo's, um dem Tone seinen vollen Glanz zu bewahren, sich des Stimmbogens zur Ausgleichung zu bedienen.

Il n'est pas difficile de descendre ces notes au moyen des lèvres, mais c'est au prix de la qualité du son. Il vaut donc mieux, dans les mouvements lents, pour conserver au son tout son éclat, se servir de la coulisse d'accord comme compensateur.

Position of the Mouthpiece on the Lips.

The mouthpiece should be placed in the middle of the lips, two-thirds on the lower lip, and one-third on the upper lip. At any rate, this is the position which I myself have adopted, and which I believe to be the best.

Horn players generally place the mouthpiece two-thirds on the upper lip and one-third on the lower, which is precisely the reverse of what I have just recommended for the cornet; but it must not be forgotten that great difference exists in the formation of this instrument as well as in the method of holding it, and that which may admirably suit the horn, is attended with very bad results when applied to the cornet. What, after all, is the principal object as regards the position of the cornet? Why, that it should be perfectly horizontal. Well, then, if the mouthpiece were placed as though the performer were playing the horn, the instrument would be in a falling position, resembling that of the clarinet.

Some teachers make a point of changing the position of the mouthpiece previously adopted by the pupils who apply to them. I have seldom known this method to succeed. To my own knowledge, several players, already possessed of remarkable talent, have attempted what we call at the Conservatoire, the "orthopedic system," which consists in rectifying and correcting the wrong placing of the mouthpiece. I consider it my duty to say that these artists, after having wasted several years in uselessly trying the system in question, were compelled to return to their primitive mode of placing the mouthpiece, not one of them having obtained any advantage, while some of them were no longer able to play at all.

Stellung des Mundstücks auf den Lippen.

Das Mundstück soll in der Mitte des Mundes stehen, zwei Drittel auf der Unterlippe, und ein Drittel auf der Oberlippe; das ist wenigstens die Stellung, die ich für mich selbst angenommen habe, und die ich für die beste halte.

Die Hornisten setzen in der Regel zwei Drittel auf die Oberlippe und ein Drittel auf die Unterlippe, was gerade das Gegentheil wäre von dem, was ich so eben vom Cornet gesagt habe; man muss aber nicht vergessen, dass es in der Bauart des Instruments, wie in der Art, es zu halten, grosse Verschiedenheiten giebt, und was dem Horne sehr wohl zusagen kann, ist bei dem Cornet à pistons von einer schlechten Wirkung. Was soll man also von der Haltung des Cornet à pistons wünschen? dass sie horizontal sei. Wenn man nun das Mundstück so stellt, wie man es beim Horne gewöhnt ist, so erhält das Instrument die Richtung des Falles, als ob man Clarinette bliese.

Es giebt Lehrer, welche die Gewohnheit haben, den Ansatz des Mundstückes bei allen Schülern, die sich an sie wenden, zu verändern. Ich habe selten dieses System mit Erfolg angewandt gesehen. Mehrere Künstler meiner Bekanntschaft, die schon ein beachtungswerthes Talent besassen, haben versucht, was wir am Conservatorium "*le système orthopédique*" nennen, welches darin besteht, den schlechten Ansatz des Mundstücks zu verbessern. Ich muss sagen, dass diese Künstler, nachdem sie mehrere Jahre unnützer Arbeit nach diesem Systeme verloren hatten, gezwungen waren, ihr Mundstück wieder wie früher anzusetzen, denn Niemand hatte ein gutes Resultat erhalten. Einige sogar konnten gar nicht mehr blasen.

Position de l'embouchure sur les lèvres.

L'embouchure doit se poser au milieu de la bouche, deux tiers sur la lèvre inférieure et un tiers sur la lèvre supérieure, c'est du moins la position que j'ai adoptée pour moi-même, et que je crois la meilleure.

Les cornistes posent généralement l'embouchure deux tiers sur la lèvre supérieure et un tiers sur la lèvre inférieure, ce qui est justement le contraire de ce que je viens d'indiquer pour le cornet; mais il ne faut pas oublier qu'il y a de grandes différences dans la conformation de l'instrument comme dans la manière de le tenir; et ce qui peut très-bien convenir au cor est d'un mauvais effet avec le cornet. Ainsi, que doit-on désirer dans la position du cornet à pistons? qu'il soit bien horizontal; eh bien, si on plaçait l'embouchure comme on a coutume de le faire pour le cor, l'instrument aurait une tendance à tomber, comme si on jouait de la clarinette.

Il y a des professeurs qui ont pour habitude de changer la position d'embouchure de tous les élèves qui s'adressent à eux. J'ai rarement vu ce système réussir; à ma connaissance, plusieurs artistes, possédant déjà un talent remarquable, ont essayé de ce que nous appelons au Conservatoire le système orthopédique, lequel consiste à redresser les embouchures mal placées. Je dois dire que ces mêmes artistes, après avoir perdu plusieurs années à travailler inutilement d'après ce système, furent obligés d'en revenir à placer leur embouchure dans la position primitive, car aucun n'avait obtenu de bons résultats, quelques-uns même ne pouvaient plus jouer du tout.

From all this I conclude that when a player has commenced his studies faultily, he must, of course, endeavor to improve himself, but must not change the position of his mouthpiece, especially if he has already attained a certain degree of proficiency, it being a known fact that there is no lack of performers who play perfectly, and who even possess a most beautiful tone, and who, nevertheless, place their mouthpiece at the side, and even at the corners of the mouth. All that can be done is to beware of acquiring this faulty habit. In short, there is no absolute rule for the position of the mouthpiece, for everything depends upon the formation of the mouth and the regularity of the teeth.

The mouthpiece, once placed, must not be moved either for ascending or descending passages. It would be impossible to execute certain passages if the performer were compelled to change the position of the mouthpiece whenever he wished to take a low note after a high one in rapid succession.

In order to produce the higher notes, it is necessary to press the instrument against the lips, so as to produce an amount of tension proportionate to the needs of the note to be produced; the lips being thus stretched, the vibrations are shorter, and the sounds are consequently of a higher nature.

For descending passages it is necessary to apply the mouthpiece more lightly, in order to allow a larger opening for the passage of air. The vibrations then become slower owing to the relaxation of the muscles, and lower sounds are thus obtained in proportion to the extent to which the lips are opened.

The lips must never be protruded. On the contrary, the corners of the mouth must be drawn down, enabling a freer, more open tone production. When the lips begin to tire the performer should never force his tones. He should then play more piano, because with continued loud playing the lips swell, and at last it becomes impossible to emit a note. The performer should cease to play the moment the lips begin to feel weak and fatigued; in fact, it is folly to continue playing under such circumstances, as it might lead to an affection of the lip which might take a long time to cure.

Method of Striking or Commencing the Tone.

It should never be lost sight of, that the expression *coup de langue* (stroke of the tongue) is merely a conventional expression; the tongue does not strike; on the contrary, it performs a retrograde movement; it simply supplies the place of a valve.

This circumstance should be well borne in mind before placing the mouthpiece on the lips. The tongue ought to be placed against the teeth of the upper jaw in such a way that the mouth should be hermetically sealed. As the tongue recedes, the column of air which was pressing against it is precipitated violently into the mouthpiece and causes the sound.

Ich habe daraus den Schluss gezogen, dass, wenn ein Künstler einmal schlecht angefangen hat, er nur bestrebt sein soll, sich zu vervollkommnen, nicht aber seinen Ansatz zu wechseln, besonders wenn er bereits eine gewisse Geschicklichkeit erreicht hat, denn es fehlt nicht an Virtuosen, die vortrefflich blasen und einen sehr schönen Ton haben, und doch ihr Mundstück auf die Seite, ja sogar in den Winkel des Mundes setzen. Alles, was man thun kann, ist, sich vor diesem Fehler zu hüten. Alles in Allem, um mich kurz zu fassen: Es giebt keine absolute Regel für den Ansatz des Mundstücks, denn Alles hängt von der Bildung des Mundes, wie von der Regelmässigkeit der Zähne ab.

Ist das Mundstück einmal angesetzt, so darf es nicht verschoben werden, weder bei höheren noch bei tieferen Tönen. Man muss diese Resultate durch die Biegsamkeit der Lippen erzielen. Es wäre unmöglich, gewisse Passagen auszuführen, wenn man gezwungen wäre, bei einem schnellen Uebergange von einem hohen nach einem tiefen Tone den Ansatz zu wechseln.

Um die hohen Töne hervorzubringen, ist es erforderlich, einen gewissen Druck auf die Lippen auszuüben, und zwar der Art, um ihnen eine Spannung zu verleihen, die im Verhältniss zu der Höhe der Note steht, welche man zu erhalten wünscht; sind die Lippen in dieser Weise gespannt, so werden die Vibrationen kürzer, und folgerecht die Töne höher.

Um abwärts zu gehen muss man im Gegentheil das Mundstück leichter ansetzen, um dem Durchzuge der Luft mehr Raum zu gewähren. In Folge der Abspannung der Muskeln werden die Vibrationen dann langsamer, und man erhält die tiefen Töne, conform mit dem Grade der Oeffnung, welche man den Lippen lässt.

Man muss niemals die Lippen nach vorwärts führen; im Gegentheil muss man die Mundwinkel ziehen; durch dieses Mittel erhält man einen viel offeneren Ton. Wenn die Lippen zu erschlaffen anfangen, muss man niemals die Töne forciren; man muss dann mehr piano blasen; denn bei starkem Blasen schwellen die Lippen, und es wird unmöglich einen Ton hervorzubringen. Man muss zu blasen aufhören, sobald die Muskeln anfangen zu erlahmen. Es würde eine Thorheit sein, dann noch fortzufahren, da dies leicht eine Steifheit der Lippen zur Folge haben könnte, welche längere Zeit anhält.

Ueber die Art, den Ton anzusetzen.

Man darf nicht aus dem Auge verlieren, dass der Ausdruck: "Zungenstoss" nur ein conventionelles Wort ist. In Wirklichkeit giebt die Zunge keinen Stoss; im Gegentheil, anstatt zu stossen, macht sie eine Bewegung nach rückwärts; sie erfüllt einzig und allein den Dienst eines Ventils.

Man muss sich von dieser Wirkung Rechenschaft ablegen, bevor man das Mundstück an die Lippen setzt. Die Zunge soll gegen die Zähne des Oberkiefers gedrückt werden, der Art, dass der Mund hermetisch geschlossen ist. In dem Augenblicke, in welchem sich die Zunge zurückzieht, stürzt sich die Luftsäule, welche den Druck auf sie ausübt, heftig in das Mundstück und bringt den Ton hervor.

Je conclus de ceci que, lorsqu'un artiste a mal commencé, il doit seulement chercher à se perfectionner, mais non à changer son embouchure de place, surtout s'il est déjà d'une certaine force, attendu qu'il ne manque pas de virtuoses qui jouent parfaitement et qui ont même un très-beau son, tout en posant leur embouchure sur le côté et même dans les coins de la bouche. Tout ce que l'on peut faire, c'est de se mettre en garde contre ce défaut. En somme, et pour me résumer, il n'y a aucune règle absolue pour la pose de l'embouchure, car tout dépend de la conformation de la bouche et de la régularité des dents.

L'embouchure une fois posée, il ne faut plus la déranger ni pour monter, ni pour descendre; on doit obtenir ces résultats par la flexibilité des lèvres. Il serait impossible d'exécuter de certains passages, si on était obligé de changer l'embouchure de place pour prendre avec rapidité une note grave après une note élevée.

Pour faire sortir les notes hautes, il est nécessaire d'opérer une certaine pression sur les lèvres, de manière à leur donner une tension proportionnée au degré de la note qu'on veut obtenir: les lèvres étant ainsi tendues, les vibrations deviennent plus courtes, et par conséquent les sons plus élevés.

Pour descendre, il faut, au contraire, appuyer l'embouchure plus légèrement, afin de donner plus d'ouverture au passage de l'air: les vibrations étant alors plus lentes par l'effet du relâchement des muscles, on obtient des sons graves conformes au degré d'ouverture que l'on donne aux lèvres.

Il ne faut jamais ramener les lèvres en avant; il faut, au contraire, tirer les coins de la bouche; par ce moyen, on obtient un son beaucoup plus ouvert. Lorsque les lèvres commencent à être fatiguées, il ne faut jamais forcer les sons; jouez alors plus piano; car, en jouant fort, les lèvres se gonflent, et il devient impossible de faire sortir une note. On doit cesser de jouer quand les muscles commencent à se paralyser; il y aurait folie à continuer, attendu qu'il s'en suivrait peut-être des courbatures de lèvres qui pourraient durer fort long-temps.

Manière d'attaquer le son.

Il ne faut pas perdre de vue que l'expression. coup de langue n'est qu'un mot de convention; la langue, en effet, ne donne pas de coup: car, au lieu de frapper, elle opère, au contraire, un mouvement en arrière; elle remplit seulement l'office d'une soupape.

Il faut se rendre bien compte de cet effet, avant de poser l'embouchure sur les lèvres. La langue doit être placée contre les dents de la mâchoire supérieure, de manière à ce que la bouche soit hermétiquement fermée. Au moment où la langue se retire, la colonne d'air qui fait pression sur elle, se précipite violemment dans l'embouchure et produit le son.

The pronunciation of the syllable "Tu" serves to determine the striking of the sound. This syllable may be pronounced with more or less softness, according to the degree of force to be imparted to the note. When a long dash is placed over a note	Die Aussprache der Sylbe *tu* dient dazu den Tonansatz bestimmt zu machen. Diese Sylbe kann mehr oder weniger sanft ausgesprochen werden, je nach dem Grade der Stärke, den man mit dem Ansatz hervorbringen will. Sobald über einer Note ein verlängerter Punkt steht,	La prononciation de la syllabe *tu* sert à déterminer l'attaque du son. Cette syllabe peut être prononcée avec plus ou moins de douceur suivant le degré de force que vous voulez donner à votre attaque. Lorsque sur une note il y a un point allongé

it indicates that the sound ought to be very short; the syllable ought then to be uttered very briefly and dryly. When, on the contrary, there is only a dot,	so bezeichnet dies, dass der Ton sehr kurz sein soll; die Sylbe *tü* muss dann sehr kurz ausgesprochen werden. Wenn aber als Gegensatz nur ein Punkt über einer Note steht,	cela indique que le son doit être fort court vous devez alors prononcer la syllabe *tu* avec beaucoup de sécheresse. Lorsque, au contraire il n'y a qu'un point

the syllable should be pronounced with more softness, so that the sounds, although detached, still form a connected phrase. When, upon a succession of notes, there are dots over which there is a slur,	so muss die Sylbe mit mehr Weichheit ausgesprochen werden, der Art, dass die Töne, obgleich gestosen, sich dennoch unter einander verbinden. Wenn man bei einer Folge von Noten über die Punkte noch eine Bindung setzt,	vous devez prononcer cette syllabe avec plus de douceur, de manière que les sons, quoique détachés, se lient bien entre eux. Quand, sur une succession de notes, on met des points au dessus desquels il y a un coulé

the performer should invariably strike the note with a very soft "Tu," and then substitute for it the syllable "Du," because the latter syllable not only distinctly articulates each note, but also serves admirably to join notes together.	so muss man die erste Note mit einem sehr sanften *tü* angeben, und dieses *tü* dann durch *dü* substituiren, da diese Sylbe, indem man jede Note ausspricht, dieselben unter einander bindet. (Man nennt dies den Zungenstoss im Tone.)	vous devez invariablement poser la première note avec un *tu* très-doux, et lui substituer ensuite la syllabe *du*, par la raison que cette syllabe, tout en articulant chaque note, les lie parfaitement entre elles. (C'est ce que l'on nomme le coup de langue dans le son.)
These are the only three methods of commencing, or, as it is called, "striking," the sound. Further on I will duly explain the various articulations. For the present, it is only necessary to know and to practice the simple tonguing, for upon this starting point the pupil's future excellence as an executant depends entirely.	Es giebt nur diese drei Arten, die Töne anzusetzen, d. h. sie zu trennen. Später werde ich die anderen Articulationen zur Kenntniss bringen. Für jetzt ist es nur am Ort, den einfachen Zungenstoss zu kennen und zu studiren, denn von diesem Ausgangspunkte hängt lediglich der Erfolg einer guten Ausführung ab.	Il n'y a que ces trois manières d'attaquer, c'est-à-dire de séparer les sons; plus tard, je ferai connaître les autres articulations. Pour le moment, il n'y a lieu de connaître et d'étudier que le coup de langue simple, car de ce point de départ dépend entièrement le succès d'une bonne exécution.
As I have already said, the method of "striking" the sound immediately shows whether the performer possesses a good or faulty style. The first part of this method is entirely devoted to studies of this description, and I shall not pass on to the slur until the pupil has thoroughly mastered the striking of the note.	Wie ich bereits oben gesagt habe, lässt die Art des Tonansatzes unverzüglich erkennen, ob Jemand einen guten oder schlechten Styl hat. Der erste Theil dieser Schule ist gänzlich dieser Gattung von Etuden gewidmet: ich werde erst zu den Bindungen übergehen, wenn der Schüler den Tonansatz vollständig inne hat.	Comme je l'ai dit plus haut, la manière d'attaquer le son laisse voir immédiatement si vous avez un bon ou un mauvais style. La première partie de cette méthode est entièrement consacrée à ce genre d'études; je ne passerai aux coulés que quand l'élève saura parfaitement attaquer et poser le son.

Method of Breathing. — Ueber die Art zu athmen. — Manière de respirer.

The mouthpiece having been placed on the lips, the mouth should partly open at the sides, and the tongue retire, in order to allow the air to penetrate into the lungs. The stomach ought not to swell, but, on the contrary, rather recede, in proportion as the chest is dilated by the respiration.	Ist das Mundstück einmal auf die Lippen gesetzt, so soll sich der Mund nach den Seiten hin öffnen, und die Zunge sich zurückziehen, um die Luft in die Lungen einzulassen. Der Bauch soll sich nicht blähen, sondern soll im Gegentheil zurücktreten, je nachdem die Brust durch das Einathmen aufschwillt.	L'embouchure une fois placée sur les lèvres, la bouche doit s'entr'ouvrir sur les côtés, et la langue se retirer pour laisser pénétrer l'air dans les poumons. Le ventre ne doit pas se gonfler, il doit, au contraire, remonter au fur et à mesure que la poitrine grossit par l'effet de l'aspiration.
The tongue should then advance against the teeth of the upper jaw in such a way as to hermetically close the mouth, as though it were a valve intended to keep the column of air in the lungs.	Die Zunge soll dann gegen die obere Zahnreihe vorgehen, der Art, dass der Mund hermetisch geschlossen wird, wie eine Klappe es bewirken würde, welche die ist, um die Luftsäule in den Lungen zu erhalten.	La langue doit alors s'avancer contre les dents de la mâchoire supérieure, de manière à fermer hermétiquement la bouche, comme le ferait une soupape chargée de maintenir la colonne d'air dans les poumons.
The instant the tongue recedes, the air which has been pressing against it precipitates itself into the instrument and determines the vibrations which produce the sound. The stomach should then gradually resume its primitive position in proportion as the chest is lightened by the diminution of the air in the lungs.	In dem Augenblicke, wo die Zunge sich zurückzieht, stürzt die Luft, welche den Druck auf sie ausübte, in das Instrument und bestimmt die Schwingungen, welche den Ton hervorbringen. Der Bauch soll dann langsam seine frühere Stellung wieder einnehmen, der Abnahme folgend, welche die Brust durch die Verminderung der Luft in den Lungen bewirkt.	Au moment où la langue se retire, l'air qui faisait pression sur elle se précipite dans l'instrument et détermine les vibrations qui produisent le son. Le ventre alors doit reprendre doucement sa position primitive, en suivant le décroissement que la poitrine opère par l'effet de la diminution de l'air dans les poumons.

The breathing ought to be regulated by the length of the passage to be executed. In short phrases, if the breath is taken too strongly, or repeated too often, it produces a suffocation caused by the weight of the column of air pressing too heavily on the lungs. Therefore, as early as possible, the student should learn to manage his respiration so skillfully, as to reach the end of a long phrase without depriving a single note of its full power and firmness.

STYLE.
Faults to be avoided.

The first matter which calls for the student's special attention is the proper production of the tone. This is the basis of all good execution, and a musician whose method of emission is faulty will never become a great artist.

In the "piano," as well as in the "forte," the "striking," or commencing, of the sound ought to be free, clear and immediate. In striking the tone it is always necessary to articulate the syllable "Tu," and not "Doua," as is the habit of many players. This last-mentioned articulation causes the tone to be flat, and imparts to it a thick and disagreeable quality.

After acquiring the proper methods of tone-production, the player must strive to attain a good style. With this I am not alluding to that supreme quality which represents the culminating point of art, and which is rarely found even among the most skillful and renowned artists, but to a less brilliant quality, the absence of which would check all progress and annihilate all perfection. To be natural, to be correct, to execute music as it is written, to phrase according to the style and sentiment of the piece performed—these are qualities which surely ought to be the object of the pupil's constant endeavors, but he cannot hope to attain them until he has rigorously imposed upon himself the strict observance of the value of each note. The neglect of this desideratum is so common a defect, especially among military bandsmen, that I think it necessary to set forth the evils arising therefrom, and to indicate at the same time the means of avoiding them.

For instance, in a measure (2-4 time) composed of four eighth notes which should be executed with perfect equality by pronouncing:

performers often contrive to prolong the fourth eighth note by pronouncing:

If in this same rhythm a phrase commences with an ascending eighth note, too much

VOM STYLE.
Zu vermeidende Fehler.

Das Erste, womit man sich zu beschäftigen hat, ist, den Ton schön anzusetzen. Es ist dies der Ausgangspunkt einer guten Ausführung, und ein Musiker, dessen Stoss mangelhaft ist, wird nie ein grosser Künstler sein können.

Im Piano wie im Forte muss der Tonansatz frei, sauber und unmittelbar sein. Man muss bei dem Ansatz stets die Sylbe *tü* articuliren und niemals die Sylbe *dua*, wie eine grosse Anzahl von Bläsern zu thun die Gewohnheit haben. Diese letztere Articulation lässt den Ton zu tief nehmen und macht den Klang unrein und unangenehm.

Nächst dem Ansatz wird der Ausführende sich besonders angelegen sein lassen müssen, einen guten Styl zu erlangen. Ich will hier nicht von jenen höchsten Eigenschaften reden, welche der Culminationspunkt der Kunst sind, und die selbst unter den renommirtesten und geschicktesten Virtuosen sehr Wenige besitzen, sondern einzig und allein von den bescheideneren, deren Mangel jeden Fortschritt hemmen, jedes Resultat vernichten würde. Natürlichkeit, Correctheit, Ausführung der Musik, wie sie geschrieben ist, der Ausdruck nach dem Genre und dem Character des Stückes, dies sind Vorzüge, welche der Schüler durch ein beharrliches Streben zu erlangen suchen soll, aber er darf nur hoffen, sie sich anzueignen, wenn er sich zur strengen Pflicht macht, die Notenwerthe zu beachten. Der entgegengesetzte Fehler ist so gewöhnlich, besonders unter den Militairmusikern, dass ich glaube, die Missbräuche speziell angeben zu müssen, zu welchen er führen kann, indem ich zugleich die Mittel angebe, sich davor zu hüten.

So z. B. findet man in einem Takte von zwei Vierteln, der aus vier Achteln besteht, welche mit der grössten Genauigkeit auszuführen sind, indem man ausspricht:

im Allgemeinen die Gewohnheit, das vierte Achtel zu verlängern und zu drücken, indem man ausspricht:

Wenn in demselben Rhythmus ein Stück mit einem Auftaktachtel anfängt, so giebt man

DU STYLE.
Défauts à éviter.

La première chose dont il y ait lieu de s'occuper, c'est de bien poser le son. C'est là le point de départ de toute bonne exécution, et un musicien dont l'émission est vicieuse ne sera jamais bon artiste.

Dans le piano aussi bien que dans le forte, l'attaque du son doit être franche, nette, immédiate. Il faut, en attaquant, toujours articuler la syllable *tu* et non point la syllable *doua*, comme un très-grand nombre d'exécutants ont coutume de faire. Cette dernière articulation fait prendre le son en dessous et lui donne une émission pâteuse et désagréable.

Après la pose du son, l'exécutant devra surtout s'attacher à posséder un bon style. Je ne veux point parler ici de cette qualité suprême qui est le point culminant de l'art et que possèdent si peu de virtuoses, même parmi les plus renommés et les plus habiles, mais simplement d'une qualité plus modeste dont l'absence arrêterait tout progrès, annihilerait tout résultat. Le naturel, la correction, l'exécution de la musique telle qu'elle est écrite, le phrasé dans le genre et le sentiment du morceau, voilà des mérites qui doivent assurément faire l'objet d'une aspiration constante de la part de l'élève, mais il ne doit espérer y atteindre qu'après s'être imposé rigoureusement la loi d'observer les valeurs. Le défaut contraire est si commun, surtout parmi les musiciens de régiment, que je crois devoir passer en revue les abus auxquels il peut donner lieu en indiquant les moyens de s'en préserver.

Ainsi, par exemple, dans une mesure à deux-quatre, composée de quatre croches que l'on doit exécuter avec la plus grande égalité en prononçant:

on trouve généralement le moyen d'allonger et d'écraser la quatrième croche en prononçant:

Si dans le même rhythme un morceau commence par une croche en levant, on donne

| importance is then given to the first note, which has, in fact, no more value than the others. It should be executed thus, each note being duly separated: | dann dieser Note zu viel Gewicht, welche in der That nicht mehr Werth als die anderen hat. Man muss daher ausführen, indem man jede Note trennt: | alors trop d'importance à cette première note, qui, par le fait, n'a pas plus de valeur que les autres. Il faut exécuter ainsi, en séparant chaque note: |

| instead of prolonging the first note, as follows: | anstatt die erste Note folgendermassen zu verlängern: | au lieu d'allonger la première, ainsi qu'il suit: |

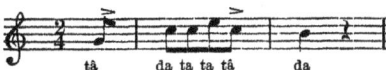

| In 6-8 time the same errors prevail. The sixth eighth note of each bar is prolonged; in fact, the entire six are performed in a skipping and uneven manner. The performer should execute thus: | Im sechs Achtel Takt findet man häufig dasselbe irrige Verfahren. Man verlängert das sechste Achtel eines jeden Taktes, noch glücklich genug, wenn man diese sechs Achtel nicht hüpfend ausführt. Man soll blasen: | Dans la mesure à six-huit, les mêmes errements existent. On allonge la sixième croche de chaque mesure, trop heureux encore quand on n'exécute pas ces six croches en sautillant. On doit exécuter ainsi: |

| instead of: | anstatt: | au lieu de: |

| Other players again execute as though there were dotted eighth notes followed by sixteenths: | Andere Künstler machen sogar, als ob es punktirte Achtel mit folgenden Sechszehnteln wären: | D'autres artistes font encore comme s'il y avait des croches pointées suivies de doubles croches: |

From these few remarks alone the reader may readily perceive how much the general execution or style of a player will be influenced by faulty articulation. It must also be borne in mind that the tongue stands in nearly the same relation to brass instruments as the bow to the violin; if you articulate in an unequal manner, you transmit to the notes emitted into the instrument, syllables pronounced in an uneven and irregular manner, together with all the faults of the rhythm resulting therefrom.

In accompaniments, too, there exists a detestable method of playing in contra-tempo. Thus in 3-4 time each note should be performed with perfect equality, without either shortening or prolonging either of the two notes which constitute this kind of accompaniment. For instance:

Der Leser mag aus dem Vorhergehenden ersehen, wie eine schlechte Articulation auf die Ausführung einwirken kann. Man muss sich nicht verhehlen, dass die Zunge bei den Blechinstrumenten nahezu dasselbe ist, was der Bogen bei der Violine; wenn man in ungleicher Weise articulirt, so pflanzt man diese ungleich und hinkend ausgesprochenen Sylben fort auf die Töne, welche man in dem Instrument hervorbringt, zugleich mit den darin enthaltenen rhythmischen Fehlern.

Bei den Accompagnements hat man zuweilen eine abscheuliche Manier, nach zu schlagen. Im ¾ Takte soll man jede Note mit der grössten Gleichmässigkeit ausführen, ohne eine der beiden Noten, welche diese Art von Begleitung bilden, zu verlängern oder zu verkürzern. Beispiel:

Le lecteur peut voir, par ce qui précède, combien une mauvaise articulation peut influer sur l'exécution; il ne faut pas se dissimuler que la langue étant à peu près aux instruments de cuivre ce que l'archet est au violon, si vous articulez d'une manière inégale, vous transmettez aux notes émises dans l'instrument, les syllabes prononcées d'une façon inégale et boiteuse, et les fautes de rhythme qu'elles contiennent.

Dans les accompagnements, on a aussi, parfois, une manière détestable de faire les contre temps. Ainsi, dans la mesure à trois-quatre, on doit exécuter chaque note avec la plus grande égalité, sans allonger ni raccourcir une des deux notes qui composent ce genre d'accompagnement. Exemple:

| instead of playing, as is often the case: | anstatt, wie man die Gewohnheit hat: | au lieu de faire, comme on en a l'habitude: |

| In 6-8 time there exists an equally faulty method of executing the contra-tempo. This consists in uttering the first note of the contra-tempo as though it were a sixteenth note, instead of imparting the same value to both notes. The performer should execute thus: | Im 6-8 Takt hat man gleichfalls eine schlechte Manier, die Gegentempi auszuführen, nämlich, die erste Note des Gegentempo's hören zu lassen, als wenn sie ein Sechszehntel wäre, anstatt den beiden Noten den gleichen Werth zu geben. Man soll ausführen: | Dans la mesure à six-huit, on a pareillement une mauvaise manière d'exécuter les contretemps, laquelle consiste à faire entendre la première note du contre-temps, comme si c'était une double croche, au lieu de donner la même valeur aux deux notes qui le composent. On doit exécuter ainsi: |

| and not as is indicated in the following example: | und nicht wie das folgende Beispiel zeigt: | et non comme l'indique l'exemple suivant: |

In the execution of syncopated passages there also prevails a radical defect, especially to be found among military bandsmen. It consists in accenting the second half of the sycopated note.

A syncopated passage should be executed by pronouncing:

and not:

There is no reason why the middle of a syncope should be performed with greater force than the commencement of the same note. Its essential needs require that the starting point, so to say, should be distinctly heard, and that the note should be sustained throughout its entire value, without increasing its volume toward the middle.

The following illustration must be executed with mechanical equality by pronouncing without pressure:

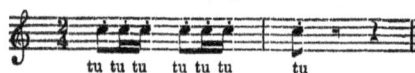

Moreover, it must be observed that the first eighth note should be separated from the two sixteenths, as if a sixteenth rest was placed between them. For instance:

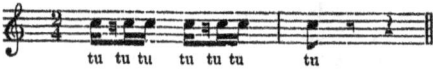

and not, as is often the case, by dragging the first note and producing faulty tonguing as shown herewith:

Later on the student will learn to perform the same passages with the correct tonguing, but at first the tongue must be trained to express lightly every variety of rhythm, without making use of this kind of articulation.

In addition to the faults of rhythm, just pointed out, there exist many other defects, almost all of which may be attributed to ill-directed ambition, doubtful taste, or lamentable tendency to exaggeration. Many players imagine that they are exhibiting intense feeling when they increase the volume of tones by spasmodic fits and starts, or indulge in a tremolo, produced by means of the neck, a practice which results in an "Ou, ou, ou" of a most disagreeable nature.

The oscillation of a sound is obtained on the cornet, as on the violin, by a slight movement of the right hand; the result is highly sensitive and effective, but care must be taken not to indulge in this practice too freely, as its too frequent employment becomes a serious defect.

In der Ausführung der Syncopen giebt es einen Hauptfehler, besonders bei den Regimentsmusikcorps, welcher darin besteht, den zweiten Theil der syncopirten Note merken zu lassen.

Eine Syncope soll hinübergezogen werden, aber man darf die Endung nicht noch mehr hören, als wenn es statt einer Syncope eine Note wäre, die auf dem guten Takttheile angeschlagen wird.

Man muss so ausführen:

und nicht:

Es giebt keinen Grund, weshalb die Mitte der Syncope mit mehr Kraft zu Gehör gebracht wird, als der Ansatz derselben Note. Das Wesentlichste ist, den Anfangspunkt bestimmt hören zu lassen, und dieselbe Note während ihres ganzen Werthes auszuhalten, ohne nach der Mitte hin zu schwellen.

Man muss das nachfolgende Beispiel mit einer mechanischen Gleichmässigkeit ausführen, ohne bei der Aussprache zu eilen:

Man muss auch wohl Acht haben, dass das erste Achtel von den beiden folgenden Sechszehnteln getrennt sei, als wenn zwischen ihnen eine Sechszehntheilpause wäre. Beispiel:

und nicht, wie gewöhnlich, indem man die erste Note zieht, und einen schlechten Zungenstoss, wie folgt, hervorbringt:

Später wird man die Art und Weise lernen, dieselben Phrasen im Zungenstoss auszuführen, doch muss man vorläufig die Zunge üben, jede Gattung von Takt mit Leichtigkeit auszusprechen, ohne zu dieser Art der Articulation seine Zuflucht zu nehmen.

Ausser den bereits bezeichneten rhythmischen Fehlern giebt es noch viele andere Fehler, die fast alle ihren Grund in einem falschen Ehrgeize, in einem schwankenden Geschmacke oder in einem leidigen Hange zur Uebertreibung haben. Manche Künstler bilden sich ein, dass sie ein Zeichen des Gefühls von sich geben, wenn sie die Töne haben ruckweise anschwellen lassen, und wenn sie ein vermöge des Halses hervorgebrachtes Zittern missbraucht haben, das ein gewisses unangenehmes u, u, u vernehmen lässt.

Das Beben des Tons erhält man bei dem Cornet à pistons auf dieselbe Weise, wie bei der Violine, durch eine leichte Bewegung der rechten Hand. Dieses Effectmittel ist sehr ausdrucksvoll, aber man muss sich hüten, dasselbe zu missbrauchen, denn eine zu häufige Anwendung würde ein grober Fehler sein.

Dans l'exécution des syncopes, il existe aussi généralement un défaut capital, surtout dans les régiments, qui consiste à faire sentir la deuxième partie de la note syncopé.

Une syncope doit être traduite, mais il ne faut pas faire entendre sa terminaison davantage que si, au lieu d'être une syncope, c'était une note frappée sur le temps fort.

Il faut l'exécuter en prononçant ainsi:

et non pas en prononçant:

Il n'y a pas de raison pour que le milieu d'une syncope soit entendu avec plus de force que l'attaque de cette même note. L'essentiel consiste à faire entendre distinctement son point de depart, et à soutenir cette même note pendant toute sa valeur, sans l'enfler vers le milieu.

Il faut exécuter l'exemple suivant avec une égalité mécanique, en prononçant sans presser

observer bien, en outre, que la première croche doit être séparée des deux doubles croches, comme s'il y avait entre elles un quart de soupir. Exemple:

et non pas comme on en a l'habitude, en trainant sur la première note, et en produisant un mauvais coup de langue, ainsi qu'il suit:

Plus tard, vous apprendrez la manière d'exécuter les mêmes traits en coup de langue, mais il faut préalablement exercer la langue à prononcer avec beaucoup de légèreté toute espèce de rhythme sans avoir recours à ce genre d'articulation.

En dehors des défauts de rhythme qui viennent d'être signalés, il existe beaucoup d'autres défauts; presque tous peuvent se rapporter à une ambition mal dirigée, à un goût douteux, à une fâcheuse tendance aux exagérations. Bien des artistes se figurent qu'ils font preuve de sentiment quand ils ont enflé des sons par saccade, et qu'ils ont abusé d'un tremblement produit au moyen du cou, et qui laisse entendre un certain *ou ou ou* des plus désagréables.

L'oscillation du son s'obtient sur le cornet, de la même manière que sur le violon, par un léger mouvement de la main droite; ce genre d'effet produit une grande sensibilité, mais il faut se garder d'en faire abus, car son emploi trop fréquent deviendrait un grave défaut.

The same observation applies to the portamento preceded by an appoggiatura. Some players are unable to execute four consecutive notes without introducing one or two portamenti. This is a very reprehensible habit, which, together with the abuse of the gruppetto, should be carefully avoided.

Before terminating this chapter, wherein I have passed in review the most salient and striking defects engendered by a faulty style (duly pointing out, at the same time, the means of remedying the same), I pledge myself to return to the subject whenever occasion for doing so may present itself. Wrong habits are, in general, too deeply rooted in performers on brass instruments to yield to a single warning, and therefore require vigorous and constant correction.

Dieselbe Beobachtung gilt für das Portamento mit vorangehendem Vorschlag; es giebt Künstler, welche nicht vier Noten ausführen können, ohne ein oder zwei Portamento's anzubringen. Diese Manier muss als ebenso bedauerlich bezeichnet werden, wie der Missbrauch des Gruppetto.

Indem ich diesen Paragraphen beschliesse, in welchem ich die hervorragendsten und häufigsten Fehler, die einen schlechten Styl verursachen (indem ich die Art und Weise, ihnen abzuhelfen, angegeben), anführte, mache ich es mir zur Pflicht, mit Hartnäckigkeit jedes Mal, wenn sich Gelegenheit dazu bietet, auf diesen Gegenstand zurückzukommen. Die schlechten Angewohnheiten sind im Allgemeinen bei den Musikern der Blechinstrumente zu tief eingewurzelt, um einer einzigen Erinnerung zu weichen, und man wird sie daher niemals strenge genug bekämpfen können.

Même observation en ce qui concerne le *portamento* précédé d'une petite note; il y a des artistes qui ne peuvent pas faire quatre notes sans y introduire un ou deux *portamento*: c'est là une manière déplorable qu'il convient de signaler, ainsi que l'abus du gruppetto.

En terminant le paragraphe où j'ai passé en revue les défauts les plus saillants et les plus fréquents qu'engendre un mauvais style (en indiquant la manière d'y remédier), je prends l'engagement de revenir avec insistance sur ce sujet chaque fois que s'en présentera l'occasion. Les mauvaises habitudes sont généralement trop enracinées chez les musiciens qui jouent des instruments de cuivre, pour céder à un seul avertissement, et on ne saurait leur faire une assez rude guerre.

Explanatory Comments on The First Studies.

No. 1. Commence or "strike" the sound by pronouncing the syllable "Tu;" sustain it well, and at the same time impart to it all possible strength and brilliancy.

Under no circumstances should the cheeks ever be puffed out; the lips should make no noise in the mouthpiece, though many performers appear to think otherwise. The sound forms itself; it should be well "struck," by a proper tension of the lips, so that it may be properly in tune, and not below its diapason, for in the latter case a disagreeable and untuneful sound would be the result.

Nos. 7 and 8 indicate all the notes which are produced by employing the same valves. Nos. 9 and 10, passing as they do through all the keys, are destined to complete the subject of fingering, so that hereafter I shall not consider it necessary to mark the numbers of the valves under each note. The first two lessons should therefore be practiced for a considerable period, in order that the student may be perfectly at home as regards the fingering of the instrument.

Therefore, from now on, I shall only mark the fingering in passages where same will facilitate matters. Throughout all the lessons, up to No. 50, it will be necessary to strike each sound, and give to each note its exact value, these studies having been composed with this special end in view.

Erklärungen über die ersten Etuden.

No. 1. Man setze den Ton an, indem man die Sylbe *tü* ausspricht, halte ihn gut aus, und gebe ihm dabei möglichsten Glanz und möglichste Stärke.

Man darf unter keiner Bedingung die Backen aufblasen; die Lippen sollen kein Geräusch in dem Mundstück machen, wie Viele es sich einbilden. Der Ton bildet sich aus sich selbst, man muss ihn nur gut ansetzen, indem man die Lippen spannt, damit er auf seiner Höhe, und nicht unter der Stimmung ist, denn daraus würde ein unangenehmer und falscher Ton entstehen.

No. 7 und 8 zeigen die Noten, welche sich bei Anwendung derselben Pistons bilden. No. 9 und 10, übergehend in alle Tonarten, sind dazu bestimmt, das Zusammenwirken der Fingersätze zu vervollkommen, der Art, dass man nicht mehr nöthig hat, die Nummern der Pistons bei jeder Note zu bemerken. Man muss jedoch die beiden ersten Lectionen ziemlich lange üben, um mit dem Fingersatze vollständig vertraut zu werden.

Ich werde künftighin nur die Fingersätze anführen, welche Erleichterung gewähren. In allen Lectionen bis zu No. 50 muss man beständig jeden Ton ansetzen, und jeder Note ihren wirklichen Werth geben; alle ersten Etuden sind in dieser Absicht componirt.

Explication sur les premières études.

No. 1. Attaquez le son en prononçant la syllabe *tu*, et soutenez-le bien en lui donnant tout l'éclat et toute la force possibles.

On ne doit, en aucune circonstance, gonfler les joues; les lèvres ne doivent faire aucun bruit dans l'embouchure, ainsi que beaucoup de personnes se le figurent. Le son se forme de lui-même; on doit seulement le bien attaquer, en tendant les lèvres, afin qu'il soit à sa hauteur et non pas au-dessous de son diapason, car, alors, l en résulterait un son désagréable et faux.

Les numéros 7 et 8 indiquent toutes les notes qui se font en employant les mêmes pistons. Les numéros 9 et 10, en passant dans tous les tons, sont destinés à compléter l'ensemble des doigtés, de manière à ne plus être obligé de marquer les numéros de pistons sous chaque note. Il faut donc jouer les deux premières leçons pendant assez longtemps, pour être bien au courant du doigté de l'instrument.

Je n'indiquerai désormais que les doigtés qui donnent quelques facilités. Dans toutes les leçons jusqu'au no. 50, il faut constamment attaquer chaque son et donner à chaque note leurs valeurs véritables; toutes les premières études sont composées dans ce but.

Syncopated Passages.

Syncopation occurs when the accent falls upon the light, instead of the heavy, beat of a measure. The accented note must be sustained throughout its full value, the commencement of the note being duly marked, but the second half of the duration of a note should never be disjointly uttered.

A passage of this kind should be executed as follows:

Von den Syncopen.

Die Syncope ist eine Note, welche, anstatt auf dem guten, auf dem schlechten Takttheil steht. Man muss sie während der ganzen Dauer ihres Werthes halten, und ihren Ausgangspunkt gut merken lassen; in keinem Falle darf man aber durch einen Ruck den zweiten Theil des Werthes zu Gehör bringen.

Man muss ausführen:

Des Syncopes.

La syncope est une note qui, au lieu d'être placée sur le temps fort, se place sur le temps faible. On doit la soutenir pendant toute la durée de sa valeur, en faisant bien sentir son point de départ; mais il ne faut, en aucun cas, faire entendre par saccade la deuxième partie de sa valeur.

On doit exécuter ainsi:

and not: | und nicht: | et non pas ainsi:

Studies in Dotted Eighth Notes Followed by Sixteenths.

In these studies the eighth note should be sustained throughout its entire value; care must be taken never to substitute a rest for the dot.

The performer should play:

Etuden in punktirten Achteln mit folgenden Sechszehnteln.

In diesen Etuden muss das punktirte Achtel während seines ganzen Werthes ausgehalten werden; man muss sich hüten, den Punkt durch eine Pause zu ersetzen.

Man muss ausführen:

Études en croches pointées suivies de doubles croches.

Dans ces études, la croche pointée doit être soutenue pendant toute sa valeur; il faut se garder de remplacer le point par un silence.

On doit exécuter ainsi:

and not as though it were written: | und nicht: | et non pas comme s'il y avait:

Studies Consisting of Eighth Notes Followed by Sixteenths.

In order to impart lightness to these studies, the first eighth note should be played in a shorter manner than its value would seem to indicate. It should be executed like a sixteenth note, a rest being introduced between it and the two sixteenths which follow it. The passage is written:

Etuden von Achteln mit folgenden Sechszehnteln.

Um diesen Etuden mehr Leichtigkeit zu geben, muss man das erste Achtel etwas kürzer nehmen, als sein Werth ist; man muss es wie ein Sechszehntel ausführen, indem man zwischen dem Achtel und den beiden folgenden Sechszehnteln eine Pause macht.

Schreibart:

Études composées de croches suivies de doubles croches.

Pour donner plus de légèreté à ces études, il faut que la première croche soit attaquée avec plus de sécheresse que ne l'indique sa valeur; on doit l'exécuter comme une double croche, en observant un silence entre elle et les deux doubles croches qui la suivent.

On écrit ainsi:

and should be played thus: | Ausführung: | et l'on doit exécuter ainsi:

The same remark applies to an eighth note following, instead of preceding, the sixteenth.

Written:

Ebenso ist es auch, wenn ein Achtel, anstatt voranzugehen, den Sechszehnteln folgt:

Schreibart:

Il en est de même quand une croche, au lieu de précéder, suit les doubles croches.

On écrit ainsi:

should be played thus: | Ausführung: | et l'on doit exécuter ainsi:

Written: | Schreibart: | On écrit ainsi:

should be executed thus: | Ausführung: | et l'on doit exécuter ainsi:

Studies in 6/8 Time.

In 6-8 time, the eighth notes should be well separated, and should have equal value allotted to them. Consequently, the third eighth note in each measure should never be dragged. Dotted eighths and eighths followed by sixteenths are played in this rhythm, by observing the same rules as in 2-4 time.

Etuden über den 6/8 Takt.

Im 6-8 Takte muss man die Achtel ausführen, indem man sie wohl trennt und ihnen einen gleichen Werth giebt. Man muss also niemals auf dem dritten Achtel ziehen. Die punktirten Achtel, wie die Achtel mit folgenden Sechszehnteln werden in diesem Takt, unter denselben Regeln, wie im 2-4 Takt ausgeführt.

Études sur la mesure à 6/8.

Dans la mesure à 6-8, on doit exécuter les croches en les séparant bien et en leur donnant une valeur égale. Il ne faut en conséquence jamais traîner sur la troisième croche de chaque temps. Les croches pointées, ainsi que les croches suivies de doubles croches, s'exécutent dans ce rhythme, en observant les mêmes règles que dans le 2-4.

FIRST STUDIES. ERSTE ETUDEN. PREMIÈRES ETUDES.

21

47.

STUDIES ON SYNCOPATION. | STUDIEN ÜBER DIE SYNCOPEN. | ÉTUDES SUR LES SYNCOPES.

26

Studies on dotted eighth notes followed by sixteenths.	Etuden über die punktirten Achtel mit folgenden Sechszehnteln.	Études sur les croches pointées suivies de doubles croches.

13. Tempo di Marcia.

tu tutu tutu tutu tu tu

14. Allegro moderato.

tu tutu tutu tu tu tu tu

15. Allegro.

EXPLANATION
for the Studies on the Slur.

Without question this is one of the most important portions of my method, and I have devoted considerable space to its exposition. Particular attention has been given to those exercises which are produced by movements of the lips alone, without the aid or substitution of a valve. The fingering must be used exactly as indicated, no matter how unusual it may appear. I have purposely indicated the fingering as I did, not because I wished to recommend its habitual usage, but in order to invest this kind of exercise with unusual difficulties through which the lips are compelled to move and produce the notes without the aid of valves.

This exercise, moreover, is analogous to that practiced by singers when they study the movement of the glottis in order to master the trill.

The easiest interval to perform in this manner is that of the minor second. The interval of the major second is somewhat more difficult, as a certain movement of the lips is necessary in order to obtain it.

The interval of the third is the most difficult of all, for it is often met with in situations wherein it becomes impossible to have recourse to the valves to assist in carrying the sound from the lower, to the higher note.

I therefore recommend the diligent practice of this kind of exercise; it becomes the foundation of an easy and brilliant execution. It imparts great suppleness to the lips, and is an essential aid for mastering the trill.

Trilling through means of the lips alone is only desirable for intervals of a second, as in Exercise No. 23, and then only if the indicated fingering is employed; otherwise trills in thirds will result, and these are both annoying and objectionable.

I merely suggest these exercises as studies and in no way do I advise pupils to adopt them in general practice, as is the case with certain players who wish to apply to the cornet a system which has no solid foundation. The cornet is one of the most complete and perfect of all instruments and repudiates rather than requires all factitious practices, the effect of which will always appear detestable to people of taste.

I must take this opportunity of pointing out an intolerable defect, much affected by the adepts of this school, as regards the movement of the lips; I allude to the manner in which they execute the gruppetto.

In order to execute this ornament on the cornet, all that is required is the regular movement of the fingers, and each note will be emitted with irreproachable precision and purity.

ERKLÄRUNG
der Etuden über das Schleifen.

Dieser Theil der Schule ist unstreitig einer der wichtigsten; ich habe ihm daher eine grosse Ausdehnung eingeräumt, besonders in den Uebungen, welche speciell durch die Lippenbewegung gemacht werden, d.h. ohne die Hinzuziehung oder Substituirung eines Pistons. Man muss dem angezeigten Fingersatze folgen, wenn er auch ungebräuchlich ist. Ich habe diese Fingersätze zu Hülfe genommen, nicht etwa, um ihren Gebrauch in der gewöhnlichen Ausführung anzuempfehlen, sondern vielmehr, um dieser Gattung von Uebungen eine Schwierigkeit zu verleihen, die um jeden Preis zu überwinden ist, mit andern worten: um die Lippen zu zwingen, sich zu bewegen, ohne zur Anwendung der Pistons seine Zuflucht zu nehmen.

Diese Uebung ist übrigens verwandt mit der, welche die Sänger ausführen, wenn sie die Bewegung der Stimmritze üben um zu dem Triller zu gelangen.

Das leichteste Intervall zum Schleifen ist das Intervall der kleinen Seconde, das Intervall der grossen Seconde ist ein wenig schwerer, denn man muss schon eine gewisse Bewegung der Lippen anwenden, um es zu erhalten.

Das Intervall einer Terz ist das schwerste, denn es befindet sich oft auf Stufen, wo es unmöglich wird, die Pistons zu Hülfe zu nehmen, um den Ton der tiefen Note zu der hohen Note hinaufzuziehen.

Ich rathe an, diese Art von Uebungen emsig zu studiren; sie wird die Quelle einer leichten und brillanten Ausführung; man erhält durch sie eine grosse Geschmeidigkeit der Lippen, besonders wenn man die Ausführung des Trillers erreichen will.

Der Triller vermittelst der Lippen ist nur für die Intervalle gut, in denen die Töne eine Seconde von einander liegen, wie in der Uebung No. 23, und besonders, wenn man dem angezeigten Fingersatze folgt, sonst würde man Terztriller machen, die ebenso unangenehm, als schlecht sind.

Ich stelle diese Uebungen nur als Studien hin, und verpflichte die Schüler keineswegs, sich ihrer in der Praxis zu bedienen, wie es manche Hornisten thun, die dem Cornet à pistons ein System anhängen, welches durchaus keine Berechtigung hat denn dies Instrument ist eines der vollkommensten und vollständigsten, welches erkünstelte Proceduren, deren Effect Leuten von Geschmack abscheulich sein muss, eher verwirft, als verlangt.

Ich muss bei dieser Gelegenheit noch einen unerträglichen Fehler bezeichnen, den die Anhänger dieser Schule zu lieben scheinen einen Fehler vermittelst der Bewegung der Lippen. Ich will von der Art sprechen, wie sie den Gruppetto machen.

Um diese Verzierung auf dem Cornet à Pistons auszuführen, genügt es, die Finger regelmässig zu bewegen, und jede Note kommt mit einer untadelhaften Bestimmtheit und Reinheit heraus.

EXPLICATION
des Etudes sur le coulé.

Cette partie de la méthode est sans condredit une des plus importantes; aussi lui ai-je donné un grand développement, surtout dans les exercices qui se font spécialement par le mouvement des lèvres c'est à-dire sans avoir recours à l'addition ou à la substitution d'un piston. On devra suivre exactement les doigtés indiqués, quoique étant inusités. C'est à dessein, en effet, que j'ai eu recours à ces doigtés, non plus pour en conseiller l'usage dans l'exécution habituelle, mais afin de donner à ce genre d'exercice une difficulté qui doit absolument être surmontée, autrement dit, en obligeant les lèvres à se mouvoir, sans avoir recours à l'emploi des pistons.

Ce travail est, du reste, analogue à celui auquel se livrent les chanteurs quand ils étudient le mouvement de la glotte pour arriver à faire le trille.

L'intervalle le plus facile à couler est l'intervalle de seconde mineure; l'intervalle de seconde majeure est un peu plus difficile, car il faut déjà faire un certain mouvement des lèvres pour l'obtenir.

L'intervalle de tierce est le plus difficile, car il se trouve souvent sur des degrés où il devient impossible d'avoir recours aux pistons pour aider à porter le son de la note basse sur la note haute.

Je conseille donc de travailler assidûment ce genre d'exercice; il devient la source d'une exécution facile et brillante; on obtient par lui une grande souplesse de lèvres, surtout quand on peut arriver jusqu'à l'exécution du trille.

Le trille, au moyen des lèvres, n'est bon que pour les intervalles où les harmoniques sont à distance de seconde, comme dans l'exercice no. 23, et surtout en suivant les doigtés indiqués, autrement on ferait des trilles de tierces qui seraient aussi désagréables que mauvais.

Je ne donne donc ces exercices que comme études, et je n'engage aucunement les élèves à s'en servir dans la pratique, ainsi que le font certains cornistes qui veulent appliquer au cornet à pistons un système qui n'a aucune raison d'être, puisque c'est un instrument des plus parfaits et des plus complets qui répudie plutôt qu'il n'exige des procédés factices dont l'effet paraîtra toujours détestable aux gens de goût.

Je dois signaler encore à ce propos un vice intolérable que semblent affectionner les adeptes de cette école, par le mouvement des lèvres. Je veux parler de la manière dont ils font le gruppetto.

Pour exécuter cet ornement sur le cornet à pistons, il suffit de remuer régulièrement les doigts, et chaque note sort avec une justesse et une pureté irréprochables.

By what right, then, do certain performers substitute an upper third for the appoggiatura which ought only to be an interval of a second? Why, in short, do they play:

instead of playing:

which is the only correct method; and why is this done on all the different degrees of the scale? The answer is that these gentlemen find it more convenient to have recourse to a simple movement of the lips, which obviates the necessity of moving their fingers; as though it were not more natural to emit the true notes by employing the valves.

Some performers pursue this evil practice still farther, and do not hesitate to execute triplet passages with the movement of the lips, instead of having recourse to the valves.

Illustration from a study by Mr. Gallay:

The passage with aid of the valves, should be executed thus:

instead of merely employing the lips, which would result in the following execrable effect:

I need insist no farther to point out that such sleight-of-hand tricks are totally out of place on the cornet, and if I mention them here at all, it is merely to put the pupil on his guard against a system which, unfortunately is entirely too prevalent among performers in military bands.

The principal object of the first fifteen numbers of this division is to instruct the pupil in the so-called *portamento* effects. In order to arrive at this result, the lower note must be slightly inflated, and when it has reached the extremity of its power, it must be slurred up to the higher note by a slight pressure of the mouthpiece on the lips.

Then follows the practicing of thirds which is obtained by the tension of the muscles, and also by the pressure of the mouthpiece on the lips. The notes should be produced with perfect equality; they must be connected with each other with absolute evenness, and played precisely according to the time and with the exact fingering as indicated.

The studies, Nos. 16 to 69, were composed for the sole purpose of teaching how to play thirds in this way and to enable the student to execute the little grace notes and double appoggiaturas with the necessary facility and elegance. A few examples of this kind have been added to this series of studies, although their more thorough treatment occurs at a later period, when taking up the study of grace notes in detail.

As the above embellishments are solely produced through lip-movements, I have thought it advisable to offer a few illustrations of same herewith.

Mit welchem Recht nun ersetzen manche Künstler die Appoggiatur durch eine grosse Terze, da sie doch nur eine Seconde sein soll? Warum, mit einem Worte, blasen sie:

anstatt zu blasen:

welches die einzige richtige Art und Weise ist — und warum dies auf allen Stufen der Tonleiter? Weil diese Herren es bequemer finden, eine einfache Lippenbewegung anzuwenden, welche sie der Bewegung der Finger überhebt; als ob es nicht natürlicher wäre, die richtigen Noten mit Anwendung der Pistons zu blasen.

In dieser Hinsicht gehen Einige noch weiter, und nehmen keinen Anstand, Triolenfolgen vermittelst der Lippenbewegung auszuführen, anstatt die Pistons zu Hülfe zu nehmen.

Beispiel einer Etude von Gallay:

Man soll mit Anwendung der Pistons ausführen:

anstatt das Lippenspiel anzuwenden, welches folgende abscheuliche Wirkung hervorbringt:

Ich habe nicht nöthig, noch weiter zu zeigen, dass derartige Kunststücke auf dem Cornet à pistons keine Berechtigung haben, und wenn ich ihrer hier erwähne, so geschieht es nur, um den Schüler zur Vorsicht zu mahnen einem Systeme gegenüber, das leider in der Armee nur zu verbreitet ist.

Die ersten 15 Nummern dieses Theiles sind einzig und allein da, um das Hinüberziehen des Tons zu lernen. Man muss, um zu diesem Ziele zu gelangen, die tiefe Note ein wenig anblasen, und sie, im Moment, wo ihre Stärke den Gipfel erreicht, zur hohen Note hinaufziehen vermittelst eines leichten Druckes, den das Mundstück auf die Lippen ausübt.

Man gehe sodann zur Uebung des Terzintervalles über, welches sich durch die Spannung der Muskeln und auch durch den Druck, welchen das Mundstück auf die Lippen ausübt, ergiebt. Man spreche jede Note gleichmässig aus, verbinde sie unter einander wohl und befolge Zeitmass und angezeigten Fingersatz.

Alle Etuden, von 16 bis 69 sind einzig und allein componirt, um zu lernen, wie man die Terzintervalle mit Leichtigkeit hinüberzieht, damit man die kleinen geschleiften Noten und die Doppelappoggiaturen mit Eleganz ausführen kann, — wovon ich schon in dieser Reihe von Etuden einige Beispiele angeführt habe, — die ich aber erst später bei dem Artikel über die Verzierungsnoten ausführlich behandeln werde.

Da diese beiden Verzierungen nur durch die Lippenbewegung zu erhalten sind, so glaubte ich darüber hier einige Anwendungen geben zu müssen.

De quel droit alors certains artistes remplacent-ils par une tierce supérieure l'appoggiatura qui doit être à distance de seconde? Pourquoi, en un mot, exécutent-ils:

au lieu de faire entendre:

qui est la seule manière convenable — et cela sur tous les degrés de la gamme? parce que ces Messieurs trouvent plus commode de recourir à un simple mouvement des lèvres qui les dispense de remuer les doigts; comme s'il n'était pas plus naturel de faire sortir les vraies notes en employant les pistons.

Dans cette voie, quelques-uns vont plus loin encore et n'hésitent pas à exécuter des successions de triolet par le mouvement des lèvres, au lieu de recourir aux pistons.

Exemple d'une étude de M. Gallay:

On doit exécuter ainsi, en employant les pistons:

au lieu d'employer le jeu de lèvres, ce qui produit l'exécrable effet suivant:

Je n'ai pas besoin d'insister davantage pour faire voir que de pareils escamotages n'ont aucune raison d'être sur le cornet à pistons, et si j'en fais mention ici, ce n'est que pour mettre l'élève en garde contre un système malheureusement trop répandu dans l'armée.

Les quinze premiers neméros de cette partie ont uniquement pour object d'apprendre à porter le son. Il faut, pour arriver à ce résultat, enfler un peu la note grave, et, au moment où elle arrive à l'apogée de sa force, la porter sur la note haute par le moyen d'une légère pression de l'embouchure sur les lèvres.

Arrive ensuite le travail de l'intervalle de tierce, qui s'obtient par la tension des muscles et aussi par la pression de l'embouchure sur les lèvres. Faites parler chaque note avec beaucoup d'égalité en les liant bien entre elles et en suivant les rhythmes et les doigtés indiqués.

Toutes les études, à partir du no. 16 jusqu'au no. 69, sont uniquement composées pour apprendre à porter avec facilité les intervalles de tierces, afin d'arriver à passer avec élégance les petites notes portées, ainsi que les doubles appoggiatures, — dont j'ai déjà ajouté quelques exemples à cette série d'études, — mais qui plus tard, seront traitées fond à l'article des notes d'agrément.

Ces deux agréments ne s'obtenant que par le mouvement des lèvres, j'ai cru devoir en donner ici quelques applications.

Studies on the Slur (or Legato.)   Studien über das Schleifen.   Études sur le Coulé.

52

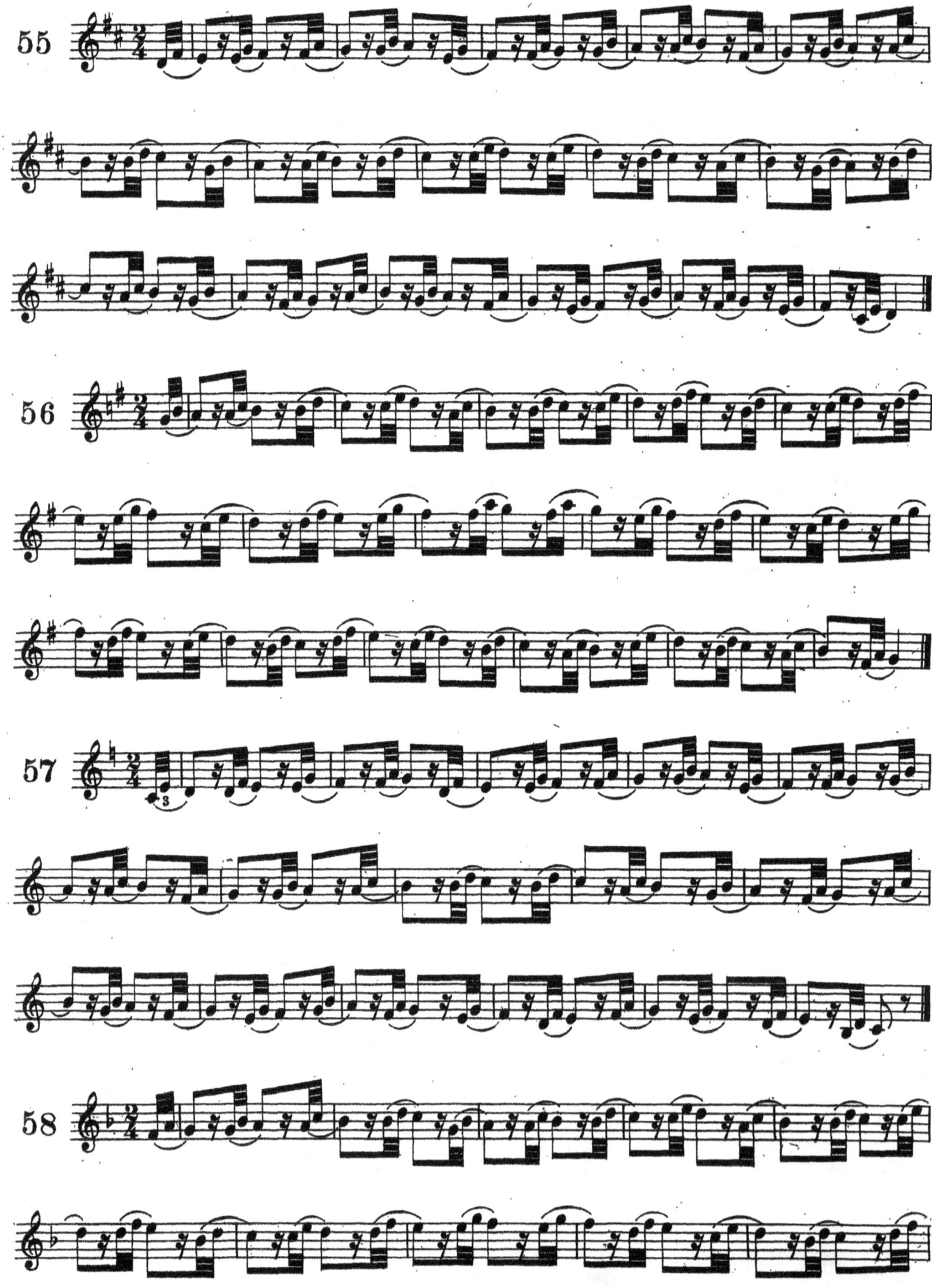

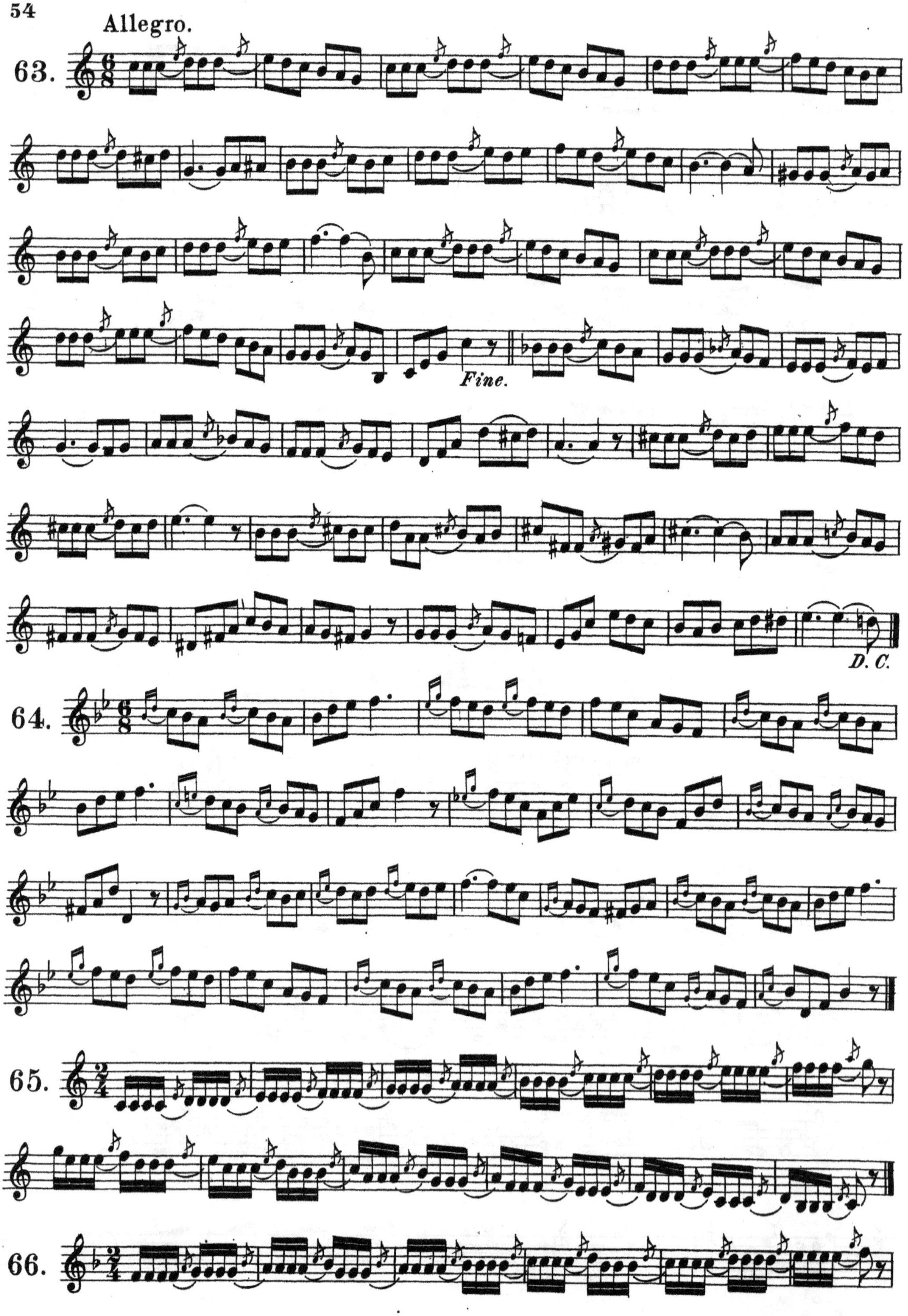
Allegro.
63.
Fine.
D. C.
64.
65.
66.

69.

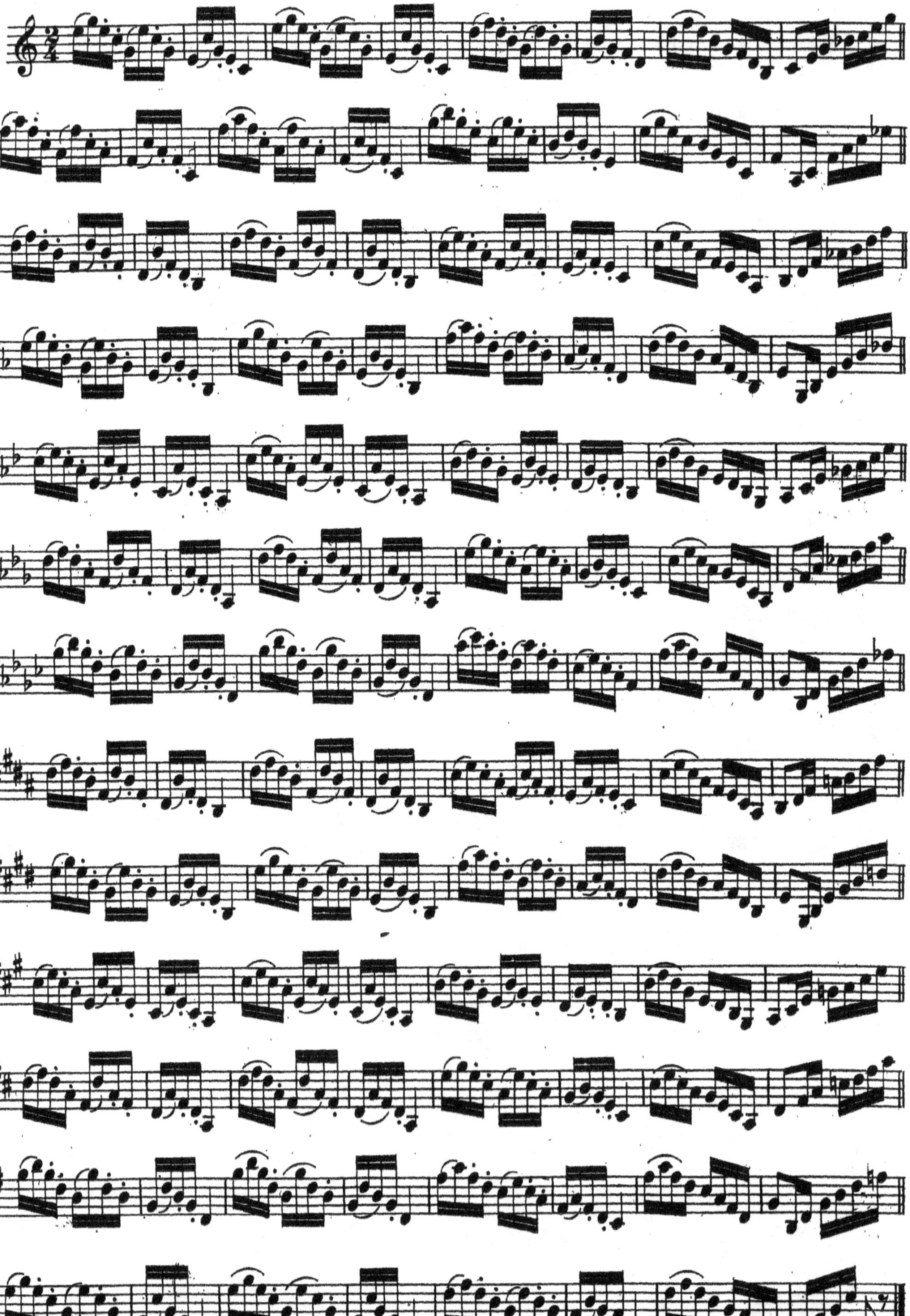

SCALE STUDIES

Etuden ueber die Tonleitern

ÉTUDES SUR LES GAMMES

STUDIES on the Scales.

Major Scales.

The study of the scales has, as a rule, been greatly neglected in works of the present description; writers on the subject generally content themselves with giving a few examples, leaving the pupil to supply for himself whatever may be wanting in the method. What is the result? Why, that few students are capable of executing a scale correctly. It is, however, of urgent importance, that the scale should be diligently practiced. Therefore, knowing as I do, the importance of this branch of study, I have treated it at length, and in every variety of key. By this means a perfect equality of sound, as well as a legato and correct method of playing, may be obtained.

Minor Scales.

In presenting the minor scale for our particular purpose of study; I have only included examples built upon the tonic and dominant, in order to give an idea of its resources.

Chromatic Scales and Triplets.

The chromatic scale being one of the most essential, I have treated it at considerable length. This kind of study imparts ease to the fingering. Care must be taken to press the valves down properly, in order that all the notes may be emitted with fullness.

At first the student must practice slowly, taking care to duly mark the rhythms indicated. In this scale, as in the diatonic scale, it is necessary to swell out the sound in ascending, and to diminish it in descending. Strict attention should be paid to time. The latter part of each phrase should not be hurried, as is the practice with many performers. I recomend the use of the metronome, in order to arrive at that degree of precision which constitutes the beauty of execution.

ETUDEN über die Tonleitern.

Dur-Tonleitern.

Das Studium der Tonleitern ist in Werken, wie das gegenwärtige immer sehr vernachlässigt worden. Man begnügt sich gewöhnlich damit, einige Beispiele zu geben, und überlässt dem Schüler die Mühe, aus eigener Quelle das zu schöpfen, was der Schule fehlt. Was folgt daraus? Dass sehr wenige Künstler eine Tonleiter korrekt ausführen können. Dennoch ist es durchaus nöthig, alle Tonleitern mit Fleiss zu üben; ich habe die ganze Wichtigkeit dieser Gattung von Etuden eingesehen und deshalb diesen Theil sehr ausführlich und in allen Tonarten behandelt. Durch solche Uebungen erhält man eine vollkommene Gleichmässigkeit des Tons und ein gebundenes und korrektes Spiel.

Moll-Tonleitern.

Da die Molltonleiter ihrer Natur nach weniger reichhaltig ist, als die Durtonleiter, so habe ich davon nur Beispiele auf der Tonica und Dominante gegeben, um deren Hülfsmittel erkennen zu lassen.

Chromatische Tonleitern und Triolen.

Da die chromatische Tonleiter zu den wichtigsten gehört, so habe ich ihr eine grosse Ausdehnung eingeräumt. Man erhält durch dieses Studium einen leichten Fingersatz; trage aber Sorge die Pistons gut hinunterzudrücken, damit alle Töne voll herauskommen.

Zuerst muss man langsam üben, um die angezeigten Rhythmen deutlich hören zu lassen. In der chromatischen, wie in der diatonischen Tonleiter muss man aufwärts den Ton schwellen, abwärts denselben abnehmen lassen. Besonders soll man fest im Takte blasen, ohne das Ende einer jeden Periode zu beschleunigen, wie viele Künstler zu thun die Gewohnheit haben. Ich rathe daher den Gebrauch des Metronoms an, um zu der Genauigkeit zu gelangen, welche allein die Schönheit der Ausführung ausmacht.

ETUDES sur les gammes.

Gammes majeurs.

L'étude des gammes a toujours été fort négligée dans les ouvrages du genre de celui-ci; on se contente généralement de donner quelques exemples, en laissant á l'élève le soin de trouver dans son propre fond ce qui manque á la Méthode. Qu'en résulte-t-il? c'est que fort peu d'artiste savent faire une gamme correctement. Il y a pourtant urgence á travailler les gammes avec assiduité; aussi, comprenant toute l'importance de ce genre d'étude, j'ai traité cette partie très longuement et dans tous les tons. On obtient par ce travail une parfaite égalité de son, ainsi qu'un jeu lié et correct.

Gammes mineures.

La gamme mineure étant par sa nature moins riche que la gamme majeure, j'en ai donné seulement des exemples sur la tonique et sur la dominante, afin d'en faire connaître les ressources.

Gammes et triolets chromatiques.

La gamme chromatique étant des plus essentielles, je lui ai donné un grand développement. On obtient par ce genre d'étude un doigté facile; il faut avoir soin de bien enfoncer les pistons, afin que toutes les notes sortent avec plénitude.

Il faut travailler d'abord lentement en faisant bien entendre les rhythmes indiqués. Dans cette gamme, comme dans les gammes diatoniques, il faut enfler le son en montant et le diminuer en descendant; on doit surtout jouer bien en mesure, sans accélérer la fin de chaque période, comme beaucoup d'artistes ont l'habitude de le faire. Je conseille donc l'emploi du métronome, pour arriver á cette exactitude qui fait la beauté de l'exécution.

Major Scales.   Dur-Tonleitern.   Gammes Majeures.

60

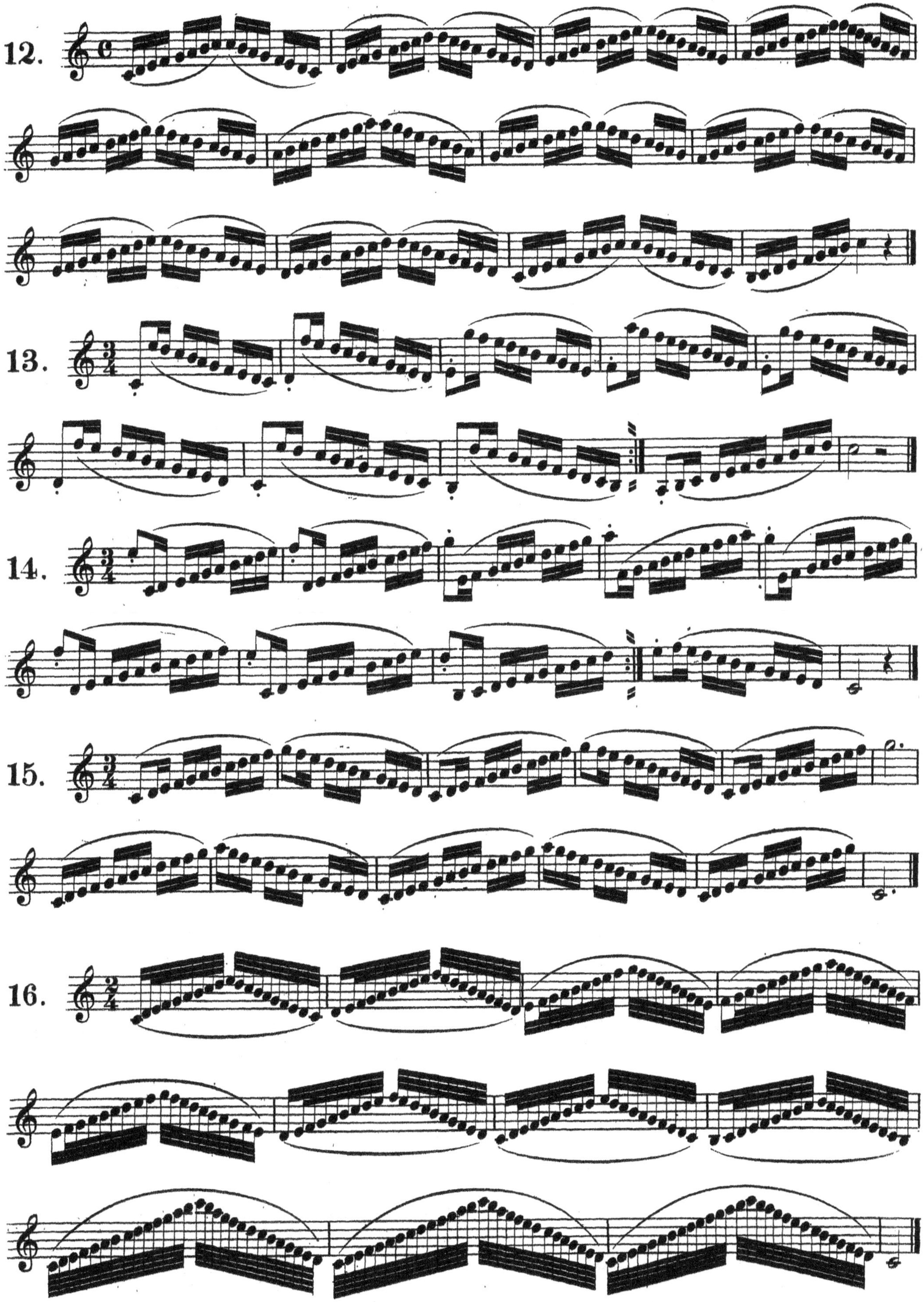
12.
13.
14.
15.
16.

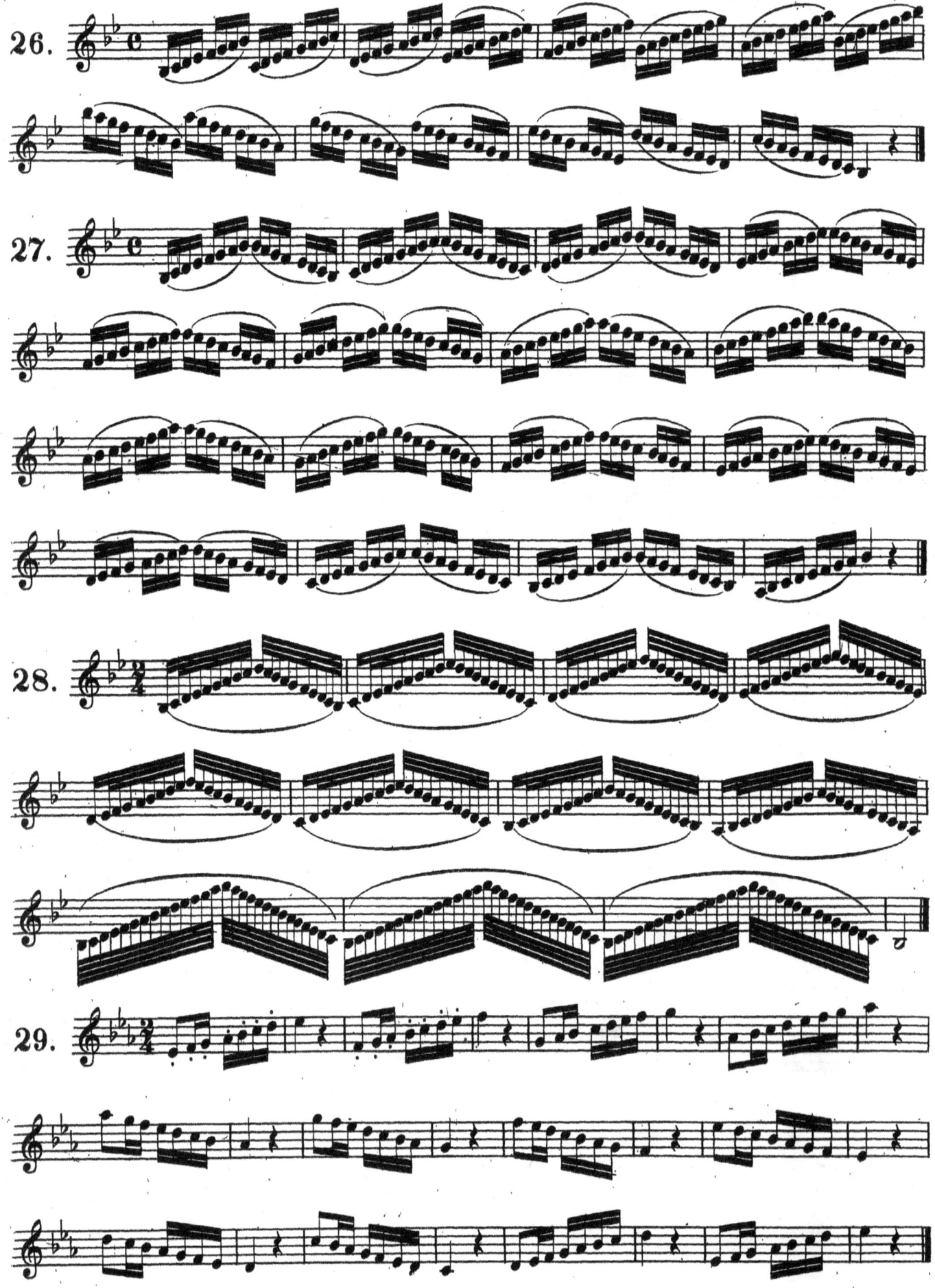

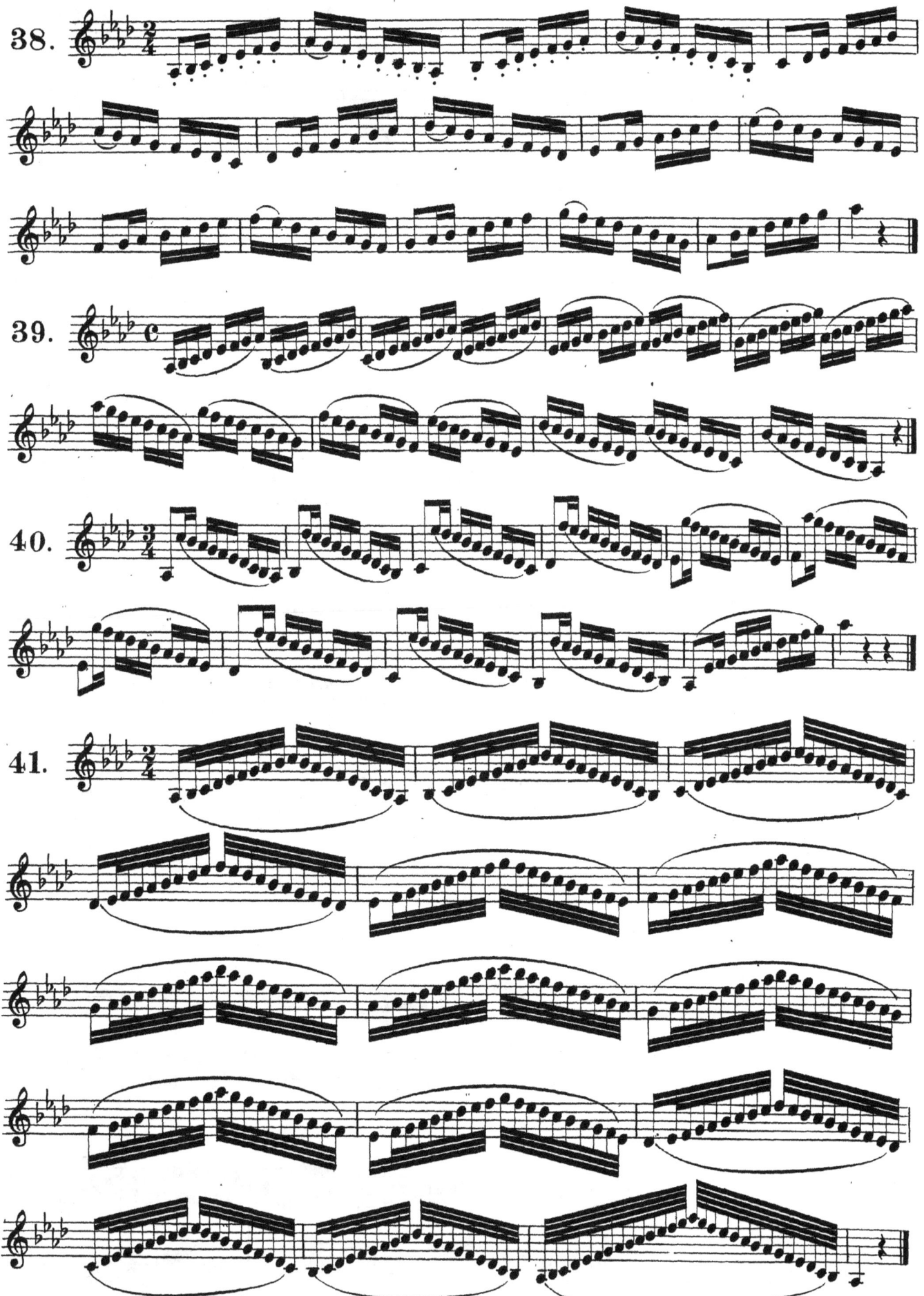

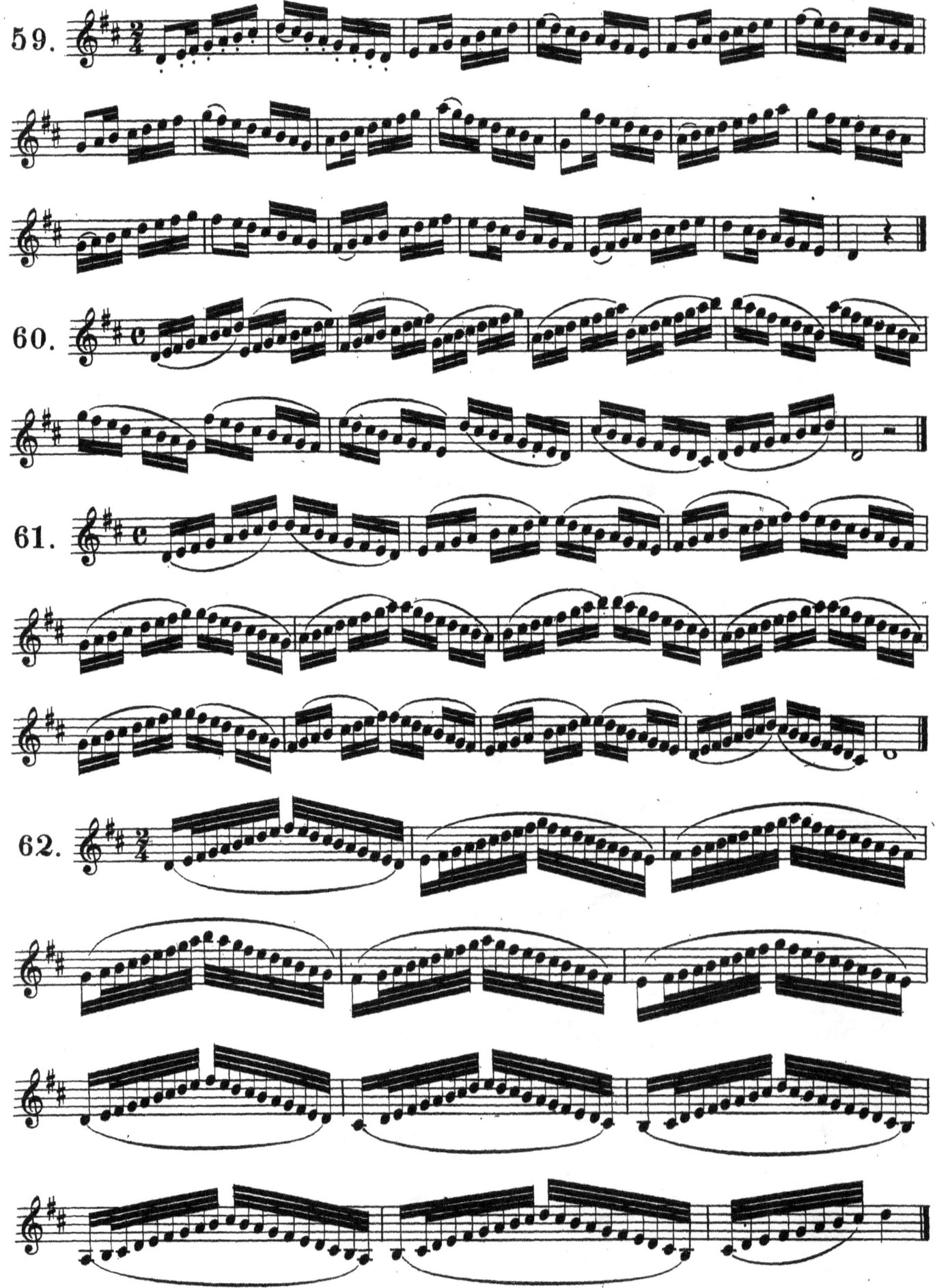

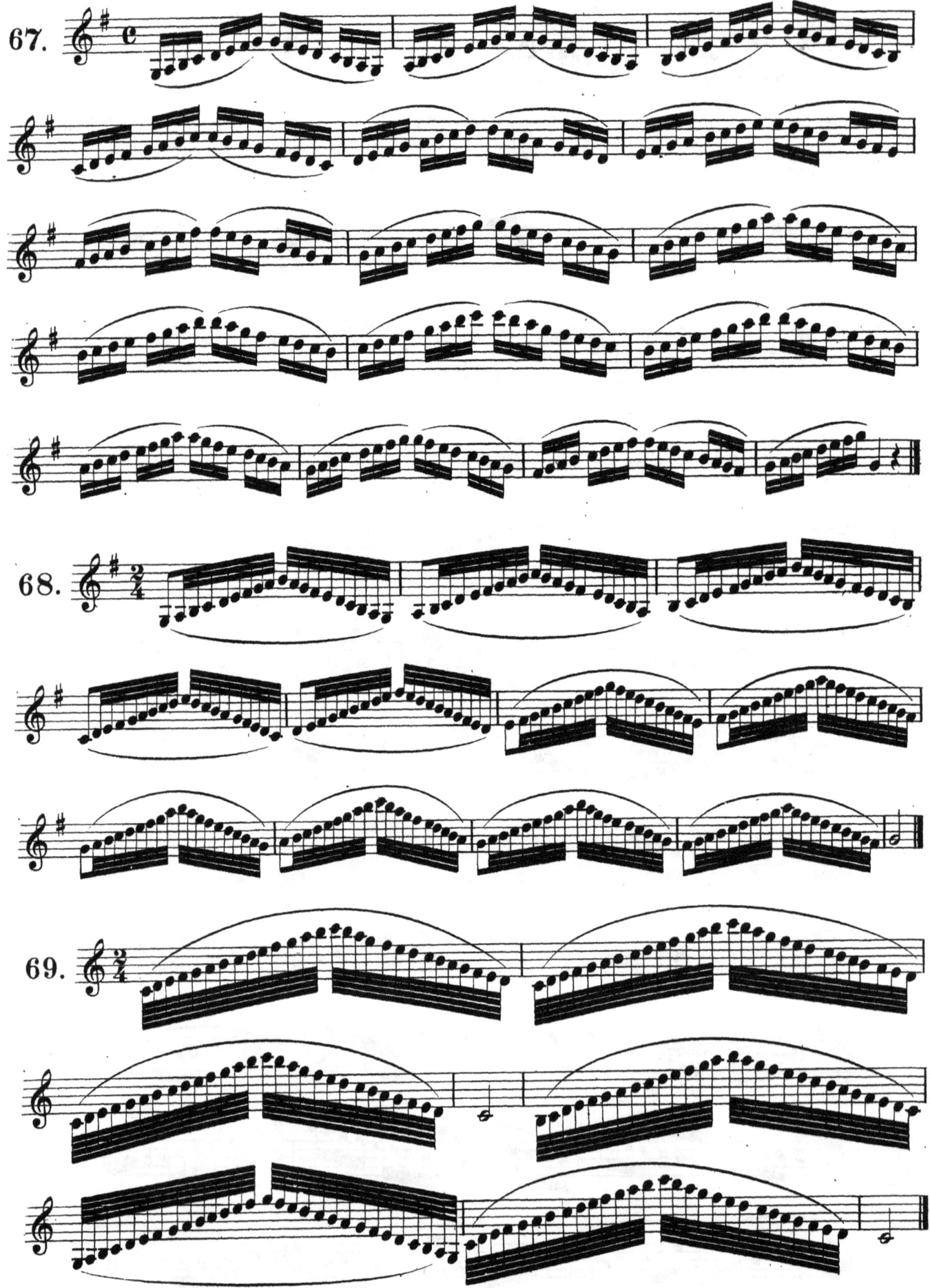

Minor Scales.   Moll-Tonleitern.   Gammes Mineures.

Chromatic Scales.   Chromatische Tonleitern.   Gammes Chromatiques.

78

Chromatic Triplets.

Etuden über die chromatischen Triolen.   Etudes sur les Triolets chromatiques.

10.

11.

12.

13.

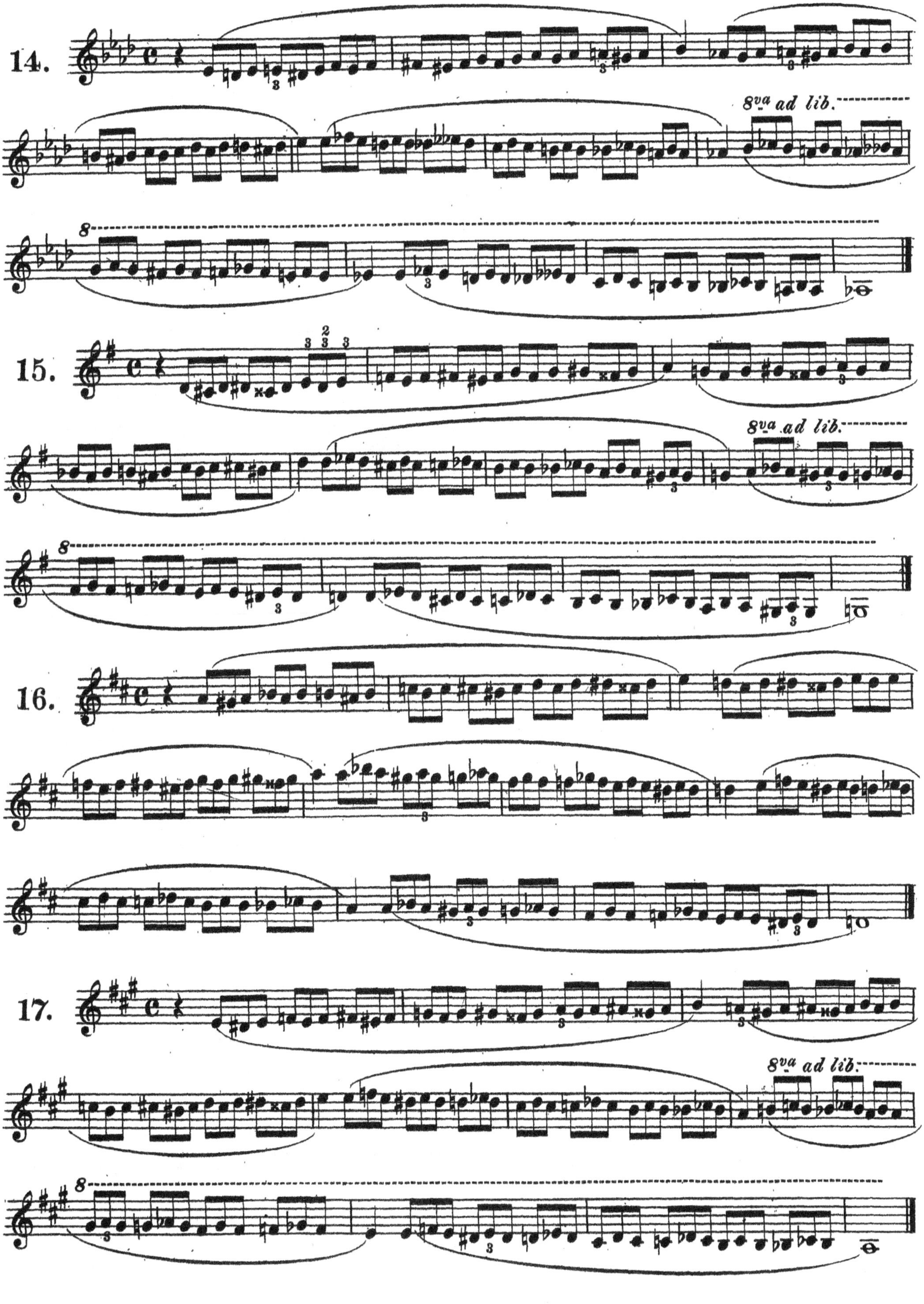
14.
8va ad lib.
8
15.
8va ad lib.
8
16.
17.
8va ad lib.
8

82

86

EXPLANATION
of Grace Notes.

The Gruppetto.

The first twenty-three studies of the following division are especially designed to prepare the pupil for the execution of the gruppetto, which, as its name implies, is used to surround any desirable note with a group of grace notes. These studies ought to be practiced slowly, in order to accustom the lips and fingers to act in perfect unison. It is therefore necessary to give as much value to the appoggiatura, above or below, as to the note which serves as their pivot.

There are two kinds of gruppetto, consisting of four notes; the first is expressed in the following manner:

Here the sign is turned upwards, which indicates that the first appoggiatura should be above.

The lower appoggiatura should always be at the distance of half a tone from the note which it accompanies; it is marked by an accidental placed beneath the sign.

As regards the higher appoggiatura, it may be either major or minor according to the tonality of the piece which is being executed.

The second gruppetto is expressed in the following manner:

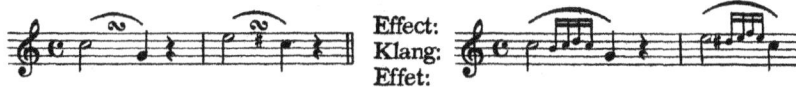

It will be seen that the sign is now turned downwards, which denotes that the first appoggiatura must be beneath.

This, at any rate, is the manner in which such passages ought to be written; unfortunately, however, writers now-a-days neglect these details, and leave them entirely to the taste of the performer. (For this variety of grace notes, see Nos. 24 to 31.)

ERKLÄRUNGEN
über die Verzierungsnoten.

Vom Gruppetto (Doppelschlag.)

Die ersten 23 Etuden des folgenden Theils sind einzig und allein in der Absicht komponirt, den Schüler zur Ausführung des Gruppetto vorzubereiten, welcher bekanntlich darin besteht, jede beliebige Note eines Accordes mit Verzierungen zu umgeben. Diese Etuden sollen langsam ausgeführt werden, um die Lippen und Finger zu gewöhnen, mit einander vollständig zusammenzugehen. Man muss dazu den höheren oder tieferen Appoggiaturen (Vorschlägen) denselben Werth geben, als der Note, auf welcher sie ruhen.

Es giebt zwei Arten des Gruppetto zu 4 Noten; die erste wird auf folgende Weise geschrieben:

Man sieht, dass der erste Haken des Zeichens nach oben geht, um anzudeuten, dass der Doppelschlag mit dem nächsthöheren Tone beginnen soll.

Der nächsttiefere Ton muss stets ein halber sein; dies wird oft durch ein Erhöhungszeichen (♯ oder ♮) unter dem Gruppettozeichen angedeutet.

Der obere Ton des Gruppetto kann sowohl ein ganzer als ein halber sein, je nach dem Erforderniss der Tonart des Stückes:

Der zweite Gruppetto wird auf folgende Art bezeichnet:

Man sieht, das der erste Haken des Zeichens nach unten zeigt, um anzudeuten, dass der Doppelschlag mit dem nächsttieferen Ton beginnen soll.

So wenigstens sollte man schreiben, unglücklicher Weisse aber vernachlässigen heute die Componisten diese kleinen Umstände und verlassen sich dabei fast immer auf den Geschmach des Ausführenden. (Diese Art von Verzierungen siehe von No. 24 bis 31.)

EXPLICATIONS
sur les notes d'agrément.

Du gruppetto

Les vingt-trois premières études de la partie suivante sont uniquement composées dans le but de préparer l'élève à l'exécution du gruppetto, lequel consiste, comme on sait, à en tourer d'appoggiatures une note quelconque d'un accord. Ces études doivent s'exécuter lentement, afin d'habituer les lèvres et les doigts à marcher avec un parfait ensemble. Il faut, pour cela, donner autant de valeur aux appoggiatures inférieure ou supérieure qu'à la note qui leur sert de pivot.

Il y a deux genres de gruppetto à quatre notes; le premier s'indique de la manière suivante:

On voit que la première boucle du signe est en l'air, ce qui indique que la première appoggiature doit être supérieure.

L'appoggiature inférieure doit toujours être à la distance d'un demi-ton de la note qu'elle accompagne, elle se marque par un accident placé au-dessous du signe.

Quant à l'appoggiature supérieure, elle peut être majeure ou mineure suivant la tonalité du morceau que l'on exécute.

Le deuxième gruppetto s'indique de la manière suivante:

On voit que la première boucle du signe est en bas, ce qui indique que la première appoggiature doit être inférieure.

Telle est, du moins, la manière dont on devrait écrire; mais malheureusement aujourd'hui les compositeurs négligent ces détails et s'en rapportent presque toujours au goût de l'exécutant. (Voyez, pour ce genre d'agrément, du no. 24 au no 31.)

The Gruppetto Consisting of Three Notes

There are two varieties of the Gruppetto: the first ascending, the second descending. In either case, they may consist of a minor or diminished third, but never of a major third.

They are written:

But they should be executed in the following manner:

It will be seen that this embellishment must not be taken from the note it accompanies, but from the measure which precedes it. It should be very lightly executed, care being taken to attack the first appoggiatura clearly. (For this species of embellishment, see No. 32 to 35.)

The Double Appoggiatura.

There are two kinds of double appoggiatura. The first consists of two grace-notes which may be taken at the distance of a third, from the notes which they accompany, whether ascending or descending.

Example, ascending:

Example, descending:

The double appoggiatura should not take its value from the note which it accompanies; on the contrary it should precede it as follows:

Example, ascending:

Example, descending:

The second variety of double appoggiatura is composed of an upper and lower appoggiatura.

Example:

Should be played: Example:

These appoggiaturas should take their value from the measure preceding the note which they accompany. (See No. 36 to 43.)

The Simple Appoggiatura.

The simple appoggiatura is a grace note, in no way constituting a portion of a bar, but which receives half of the value of the note before which it is placed.

Example:

This appoggiatura may be placed above or below any note. When it is placed above, it may be at the distance of a tone or half tone; when it is placed below, it ought, invariably, to be at the distance of a half tone.

For instance:

In the music of the old masters are to be found numerous examples of the appoggiatura, intended to take half the value of the note which they precede; but, at the present day, in order to obtain a uniform execution, music is written precisely as it is intended to be executed; this is undeniably, a far better plan. See from No. 44 to 47.

The Short Appoggiatura or Grace Note.

The grace note deducts its value from the note which it accompanies. It is generally employed in somewhat animated movements. Stress should be laid upon it so as to impart to it a little more force than the note which it precedes. When it is above, it may be situated a tone or half a tone from the note it accompanies; when it is below, it is invariably placed at the distance of half a tone. (See from No. 48 to 54.)

The Portamento.

The portamento is a little note which is, in fact, merely the repetition of a note which the performer desires to carry to another by slurring. This kind of embellishment must not be used too freely, as it would be a proof of bad taste. When judiciously employed it is highly effective, but, for my own part, I decidedly prefer that the tone should be slurred without having recourse to the grace note. (See from No. 55 to 59.)

Von der einfachen Appoggiatur.

Die einfache Appoggiatur ist eine ausser der Harmonie liegende kleine Note, welche jedoch die Hälfte des Werthes derjenigen Note erhält, welcher sie voraufgeht:

Beispiel:

Diese Appoggiatur kann oberhalb oder unterhalb einer beliebigen Note gestellt werden. Steht sie oberhalb, so kann ihre Entfernung einen oder einen halben Ton ausmachen; steht sie unterhalb, so darf sie ohne Unterschied nur einen halben Ton entfernt sein.

Beispiel:

In der Musik der alten Meister findet man viele Beispiele von Appoggiaturen, welche von der Note, vor welche sie stehen, die Hälfte des Werthes entnehmen sollen, aber heute schreibt man um eine gleichförmige Ausführung zu erlangen, im Allgemeinen so, wie es ausgeführt werden soll, was unbestreitbar besser ist. (Siehe No. 44 bis No. 47.)

Von der kurzen Appoggiatur oder dem Prallvorschlag.

Der kurze (Prall-) Vorschlag entnimmt seinen Werth von der Note, zu welcher er gehört. Er wird besonders in lebhafteren Tempos angewandt. Man muss ihn beim Ansatz etwas accentuiren, indem man ihn etwas stärker nimmt, als den Ton welchem er voraufgeht. Ist er aus dem nächst höheren Tone gebildet, so kann er aus der grossen oder kleinen Secunde bestehen, ist er dagegen aus dem nächst tieferen Ton gebildet, so darf er stets nur aus der kleinen Secunde bestehen. (Siehe No. 48 bis No. 54.)

Vom Portamento.

Das Portamento ist eine kleine Note, welche in Wahrheit nur die Wiederholung einer beliebigen Note ist, welche man, indem man den Ton schleift, auf eine andere Note übertragen will. Man muss diese Art Verzierung nicht missbrauchen, denn das würde geschmacklos werden, mit Maass angewendet, kann sie von grosser Wirkung sein; aber ich würde ihr das ohne Hülfe der kleinen Note ausgeführte Portamento bei Weitem vorziehen. (Siehe No. 55 bis No. 59.)

De l'appoggiature simple.

L'appoggiature simple est une petite note ne faisant aucunement partie d'un accord, et qui prend néanmoins la moitié de la valeur de la note devant laquelle elle est placée.

Exemple:

L'appoggiature peut se placer au-dessus ou au-dessous d'une note quelconque. Lorsqu'elle est placée au-dessus, elle peut être à la distance d'un ton ou d'un demi-ton; lorsqu'elle est placée au-dessous, elle doit invariablement se trouver à la distance d'un demi-ton.

Exemple:

Dans la musique des anciens maîtres, on trouve une grande quantité d'exemples d'appoggiatures devant prendre la moitié de la valeur de la note qu'elles précédent, mais aujourd'hui, afin d'obtenir une exécution uniforme, on écrit généralement la musique ainsi qu'elle doit être exécutée, ce qui vaut beaucoup mieux, sans contredit. (Voyez no. 44 au no. 47.)

De l'appoggiature brève ou petite note.

La petite note prend sa valeur sur la note même qu'elle accompagne; elle s'emploie généralement dans les mouvements un peu vifs. On doit appuyer en l'attaquant, de manière à lui donner un peu plus de force qu'à la note qu'elle précède. Quand elle est supérieure, elle peut se trouver à un ton ou à un demi-ton de la note qu'elle accompagne, quand elle est inférieure, elle se place invariablement à la distance d'un demi-ton. (Voyez du no. 48 au no. 54.)

Du portamento.

Le portamento est une petite note qui n'est par le fait, que la répétition d'une note quelconque que l'on veut porter sur une autre en glissant le son. Il ne faut pas abuser de ce genre d'agrément, car il deviendrait de mauvais goût; employé avec ménagement, il peut être d'un grand effet; mais je lui préfère de beaucoup le son porté sans le secours de la petite note. (Voyez du no. 55 au no. 59.)

The Trill (or Shake.)

On instruments with valves the trill is the most difficult of all embellishments. The only trill which is really endurable on this instrument is that in half tones. Whole-tone trills, however, may be produced, but care must be taken to press the valves down so that each note may be perfectly distinct.

The student should previously practice studies No. 60 to 67, slowly and deliberately, so as to arrive at the pure production of each sound. At a later period he may perform the studies on the trill, taking care to follow the fingering exactly as indicated. (See from No. 68 to 80.)

The Mordant.

The mordant is nothing more than a precipitated trill or shake. It requires neither preparation nor resolution. It is indicated by the following sign:

Its effect is as follows:

The mordant, consisting of several beats is almost impracticable on the cornet. The performer must therefore restrict himself to the mordant with one beat, which is much more easy of execution, and is moreover, very graceful.

The mordant takes its value (time) from the note to which it belongs. (See from No. 81 to 88.)

N. B. All the lessons on grace notes having been specially composed to serve as studies, I have purposely assembled together and in profusion, every kind of grace note. Care, however, must be taken not to use them too abundantly, as an excess of ornament is always in bad taste.

Vom Triller.

Auf allen Instrumenten mit Pistons ist der Triller die schwierigste aller Verzierungen. Eigentlich ist nur der Triller von einem halben Ton erträglich. Man kann indessen Triller von einem ganzen Ton machen, aber muss dann Sorge tragen, die Pistons regelmässig hinunterzudrücken, damit jeder einzelne Trillerschlag bestimmt erkennbar ist.

Man wird also vorläufig mit Geduld und ohne sich zu übereilen, die Etuden von 60 bis 67 üben müssen, bis man dahin gelangt, jeden Ton rein herauszubringen. Später kann man die Etuden über den Triller üben, indem man genau dem vorgezeichneten Fingersatze folgt. (Siehe No. 68 bis No. 80.)

Vom Mordant.

Der Mordant ist nichts als ein kurz-abgeschnellter Triller; er bedarf weder der Vorbereitung, noch des Nachschlags. Man bezeichnet ihn durch folgendes Zeichen.

Klang:

Der aus mehreren Trillerschlägen bestehende Mordant ist auf dem Cornet à Pistons fast un ausführbar. Man muss sich daher an den Mordant mit einem einzelnen Trillerschlag halten der sich mit weit mehr Leichtigkeit ausführen lässt und sehr graziös ist.

Effect:
Klang:
Effet:

Der Mordant entnimmt seinen Werth von der Note, zu welcher er gehört. (Siehe No. 81 bis No. 88.)

N. B. Da alle Uebungen über die Verzierungsnoten nur componirt sind, um als Studium zu dienen, so habe ich absichtlich die Verzierungen in überreicher Weise angebracht. Man muss sich aber hüten, in der Praxis damit Missbrauch zu treiben, denn dies würde von dem schlechtesten Geschmack Zeugniss geben.

Du trille.

Sur les instruments à pistons le trille est le plus difficile de tous les agréments. Il n'y a réellement que le trille d'un demi-ton qui soit supportable. On peut cependant faire des trilles d'un ton, mais il faut avoir soin d'enfoncer régulièrement les pistons, afin que chaque battement soit bien distinct.

On devra donc préalablement travailler avec patience et sans se presser, les études du no. 60 au no. 67 afin d'arriver à faire sortir purement chaque son. Plus tard, on pourra jouer les études sur le trille, en suivant exactement les doigtés indiqués. (Voyez du no. 68 au no. 80.)

Du mordant.

Le mordant n'est autre chose qu'un trille précipité, il ne demande ni préparation ni résolution. On l'indique par le signe suivant:

En voici l'effet:

Le mordant composé de plusieurs battements est presque impraticable sur le cornet à pistons. Il faut donc s'en tenir au mordant à un seul battement, qui se fait avec beaucoup plus de facilité et qui est très-gracieux.

Le mordant prend sa valeur sur la note même à laquelle il appartient. (Voyez du no. 81 au no. 88.)

N. B. Toutes les leçons sur les notes d'agrément étant spécialement composées pour servir d'étude, j'ai réuni à dessein, avec profusion, tous les genres de note d'agrément. Mais il faut bien se garder d'en abuser ainsi dans la partique, car cela serait du plus mauvais goût.

PREPARATORY EXERCISES ON THE GRUPPETTO.
VORBEREITENDE ETÜDEN ÜBER DEN GRUPPETTO (Doppelschlag.)
ETUDES PREPARATOIRES SUR LE GRUPPETTO.

92

2.

3.

THE GRUPPETTO.
VOM GRUPPETTO (Doppelschlag.)
DU GRUPPETTO.

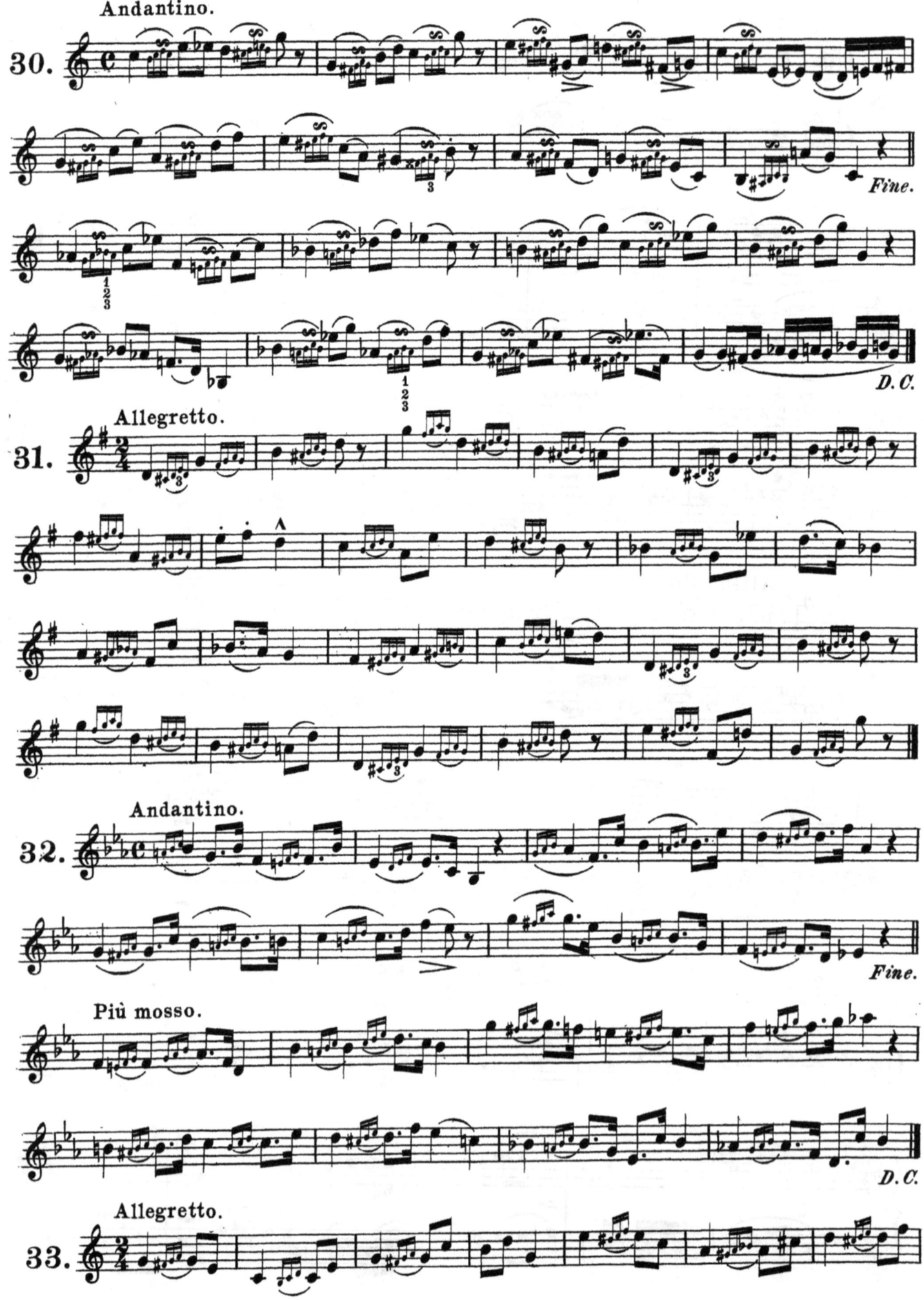

THE DOUBLE APPOGGIATURA (Grace Note.)
VON DER DOPPEL-APPOGGIATUR.
DE LA DOUBLE APPOGGIATURE.

Andante.

42.

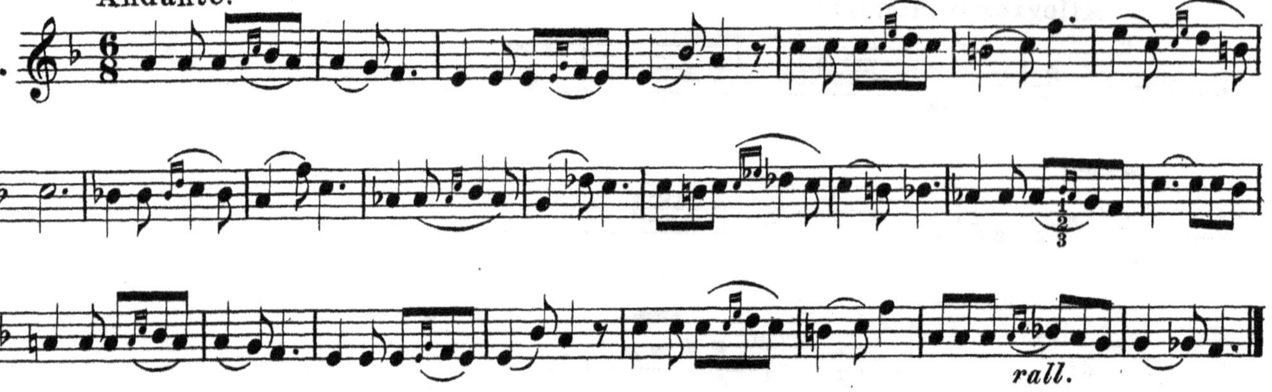

Allegretto.

43.

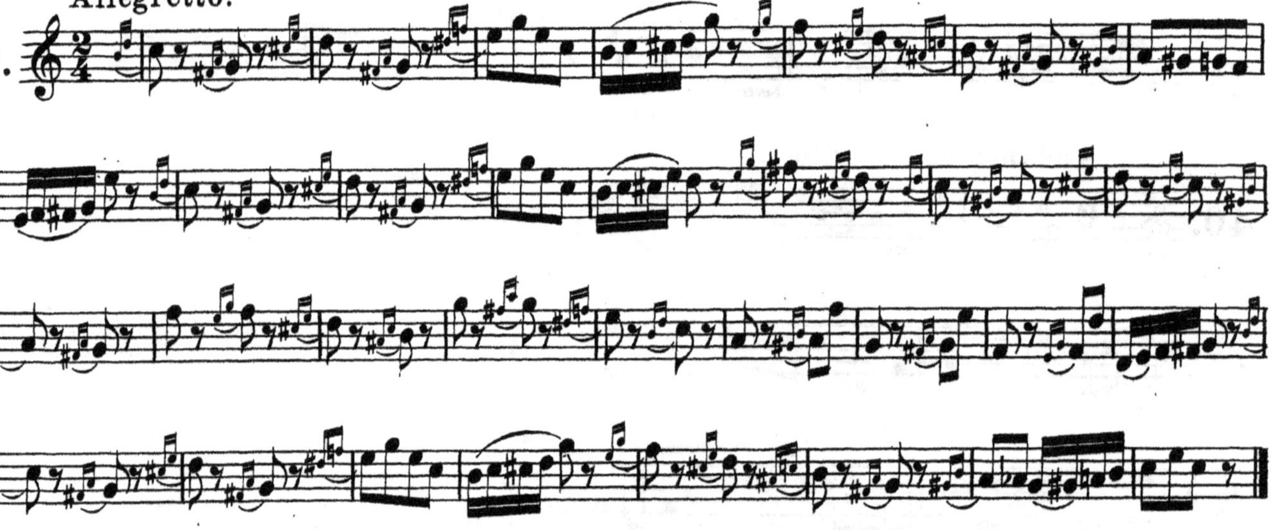

THE SIMPLE APPOGGIATURA (Grace Note.)
VON DER EINFACHEN APPOGGIATUR.
DE L'APPOGGIATURE SIMPLE.

Andante con spirito.

44.

Allegro moderato.

45.

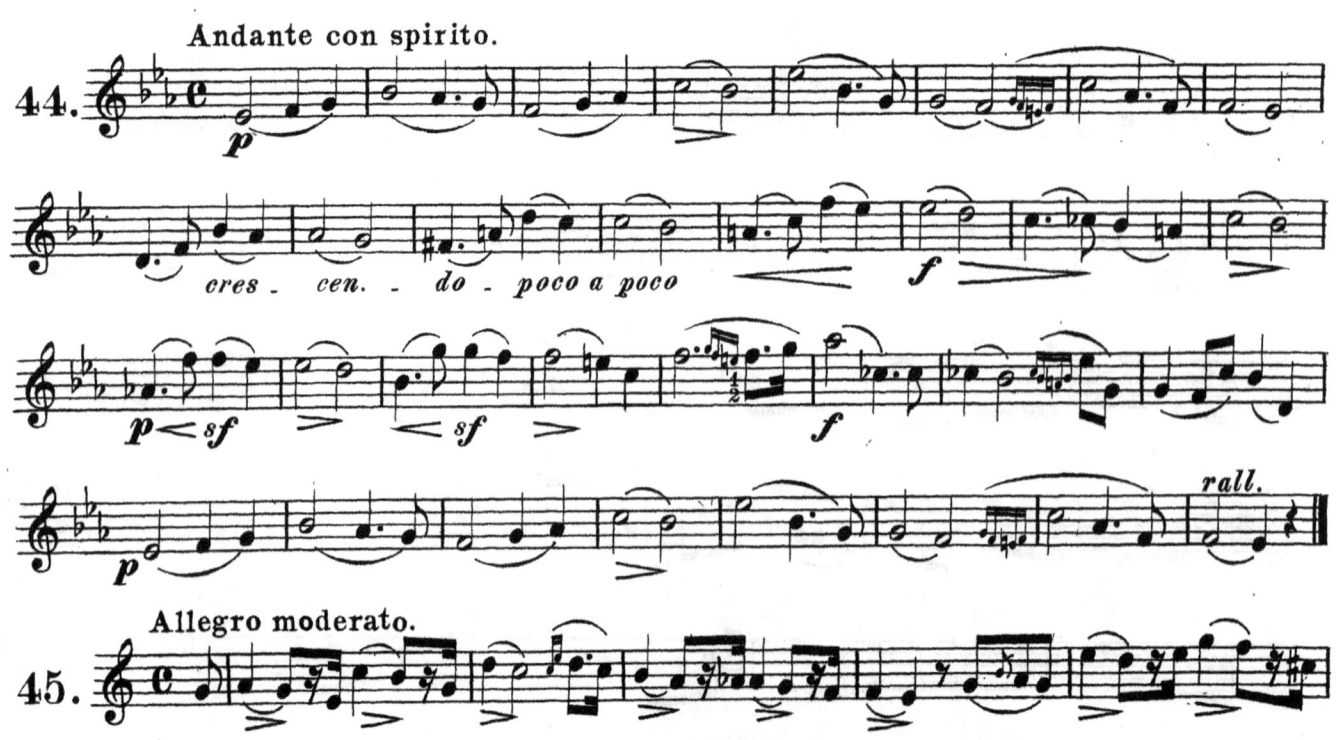

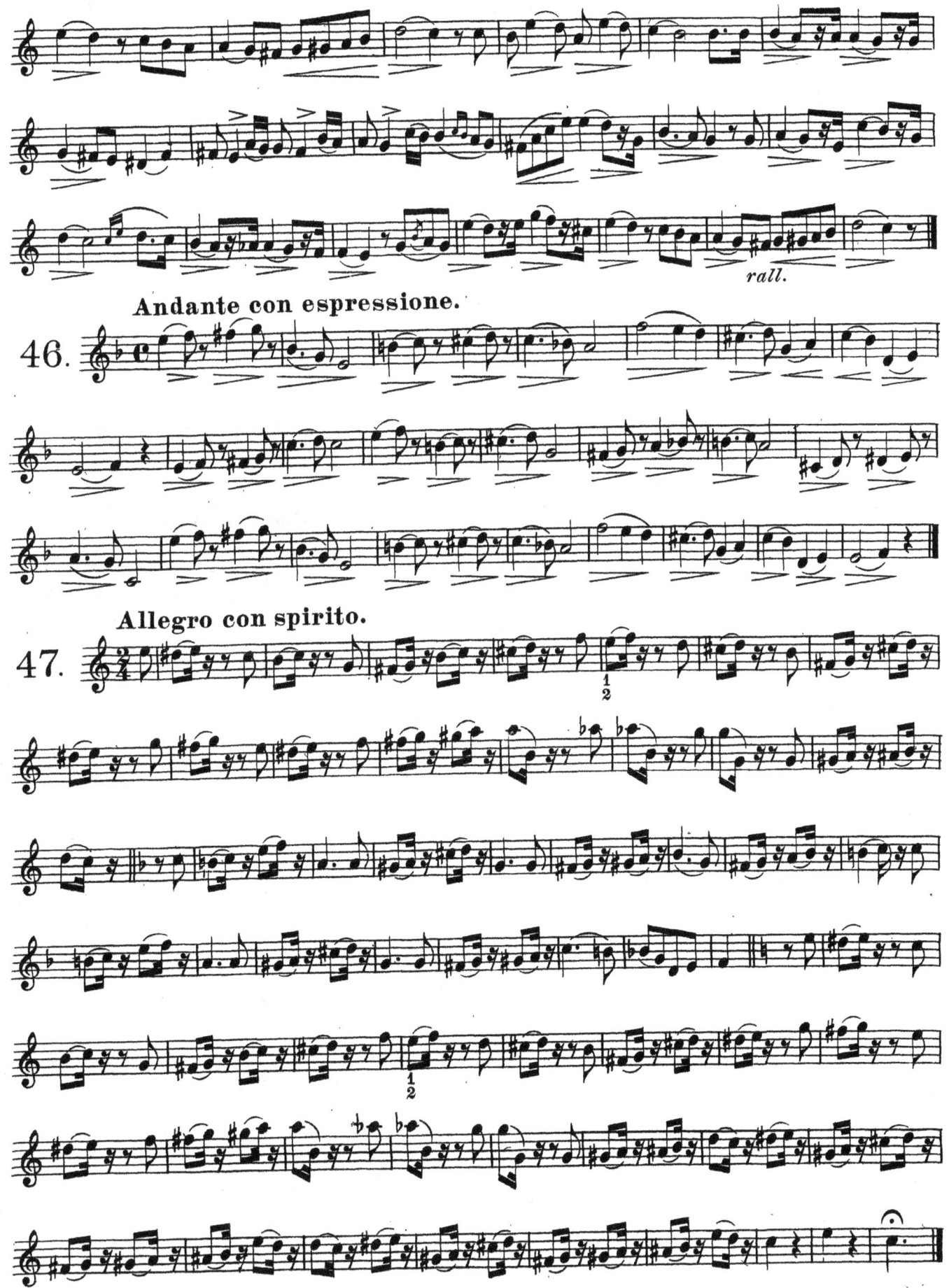

108

THE SHORT APPOG-GIATURA or GRACE-NOTE.

VON DER KURZEN APPOGGIA-TUR oder PRALL-VORSCHLAG.

DE L'APPOGGIATURE BRÈVE OU PETITE NOTE.

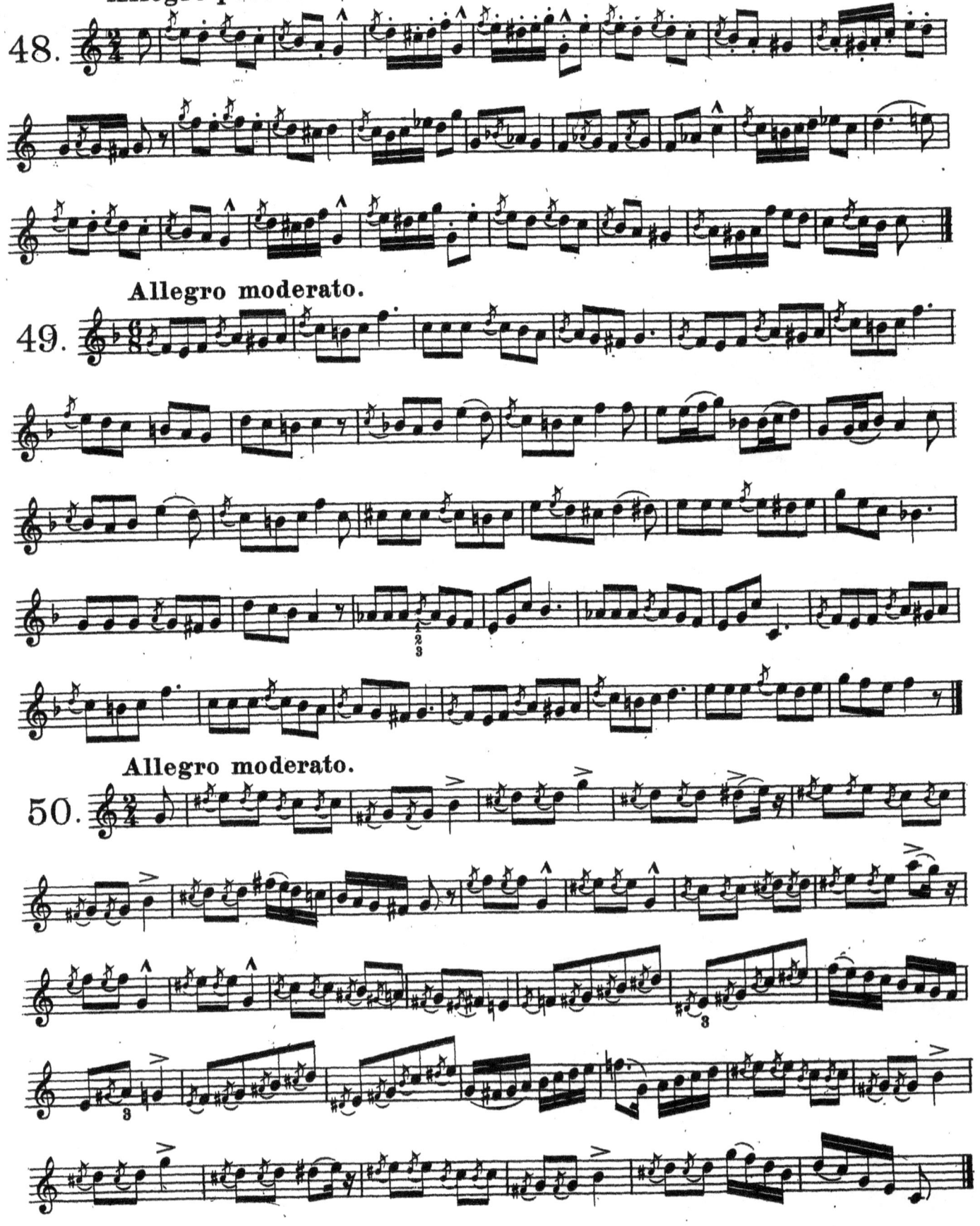

THE PORTAMENTO.   VOM PORTAMENTO.   DU PORTAMENTO.

55. **Andante.**

Agitato.

rall.

Tempo I.

56. **Andante.**

Fine.

D. C.

57. **Andante.**

rall.   **Tempo I.**

58. **Allegretto.**

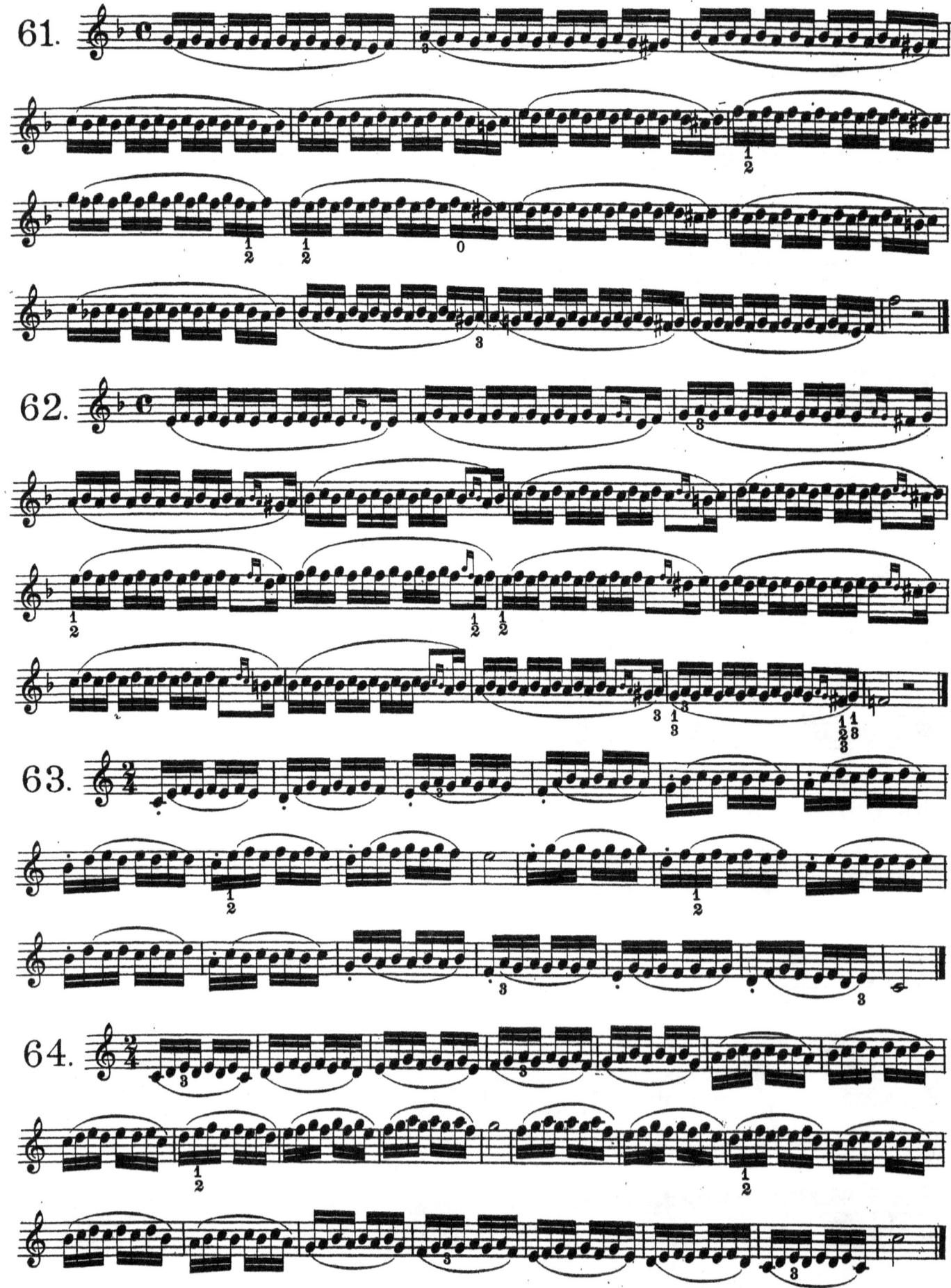

114

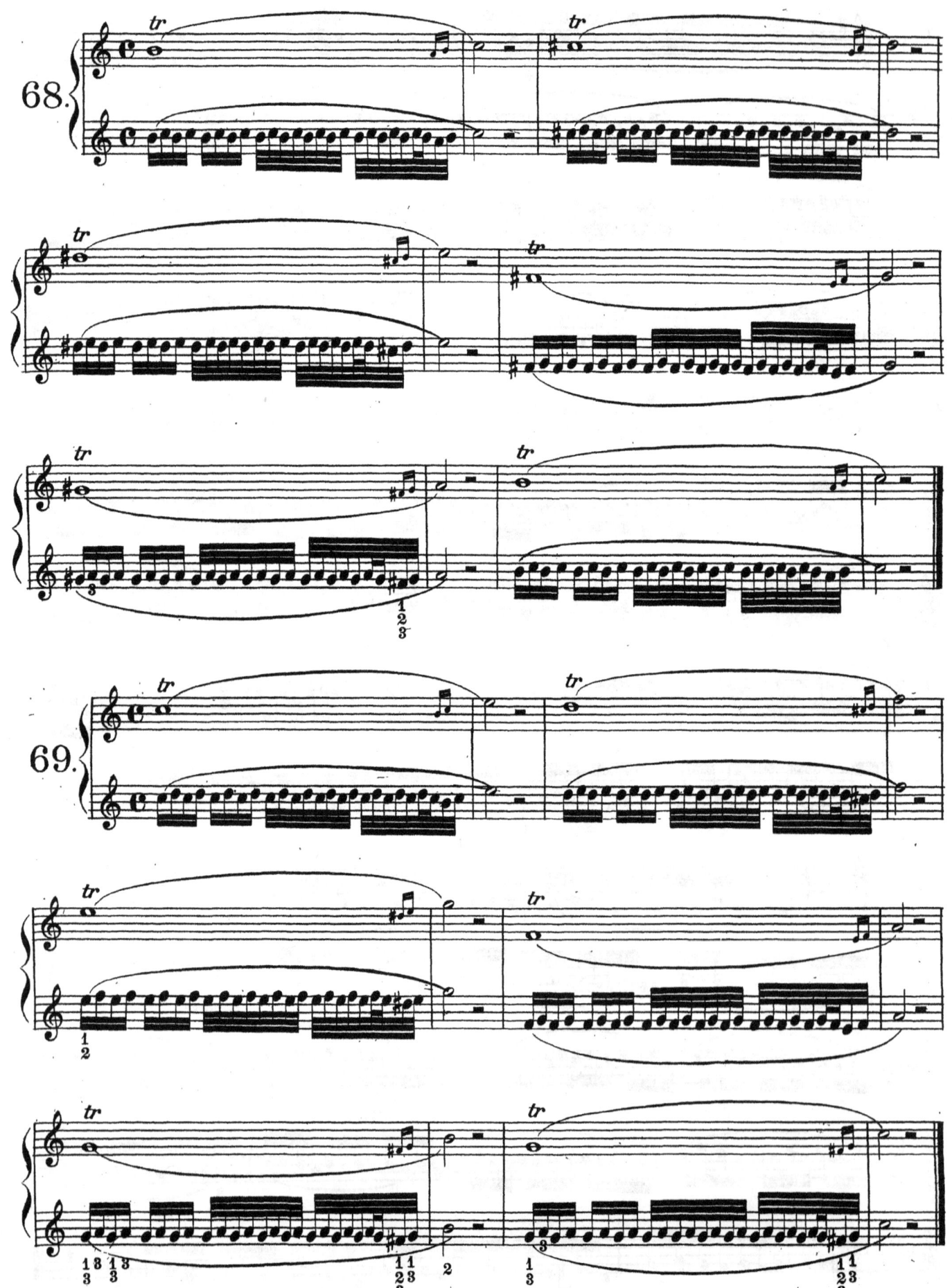

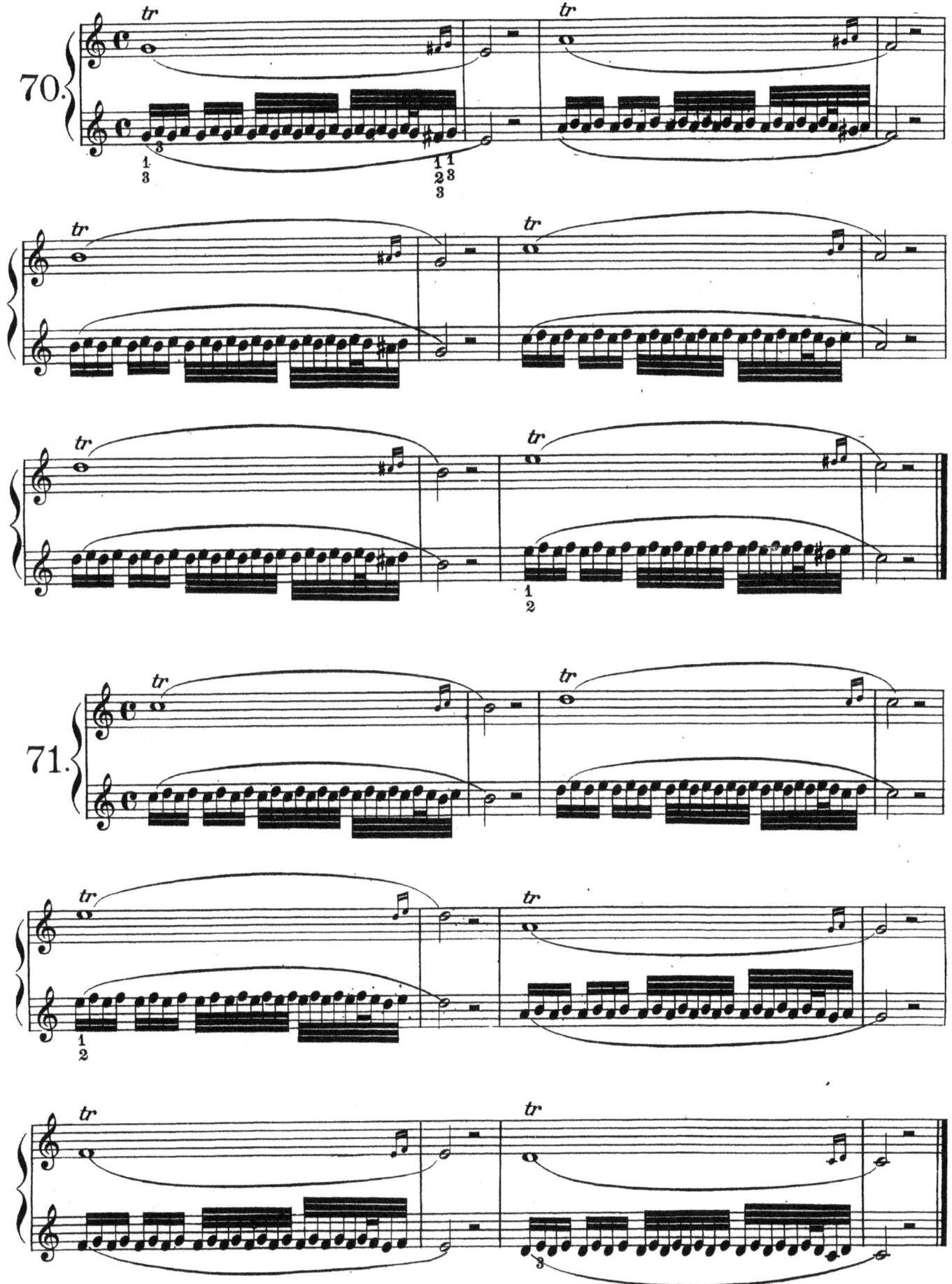

118

119

THE MORDANT (or PASSING SHAKE.)   VOM MORDANT.   DU MORDANT.
Allegro moderato.

Allegretto moderato.

83.

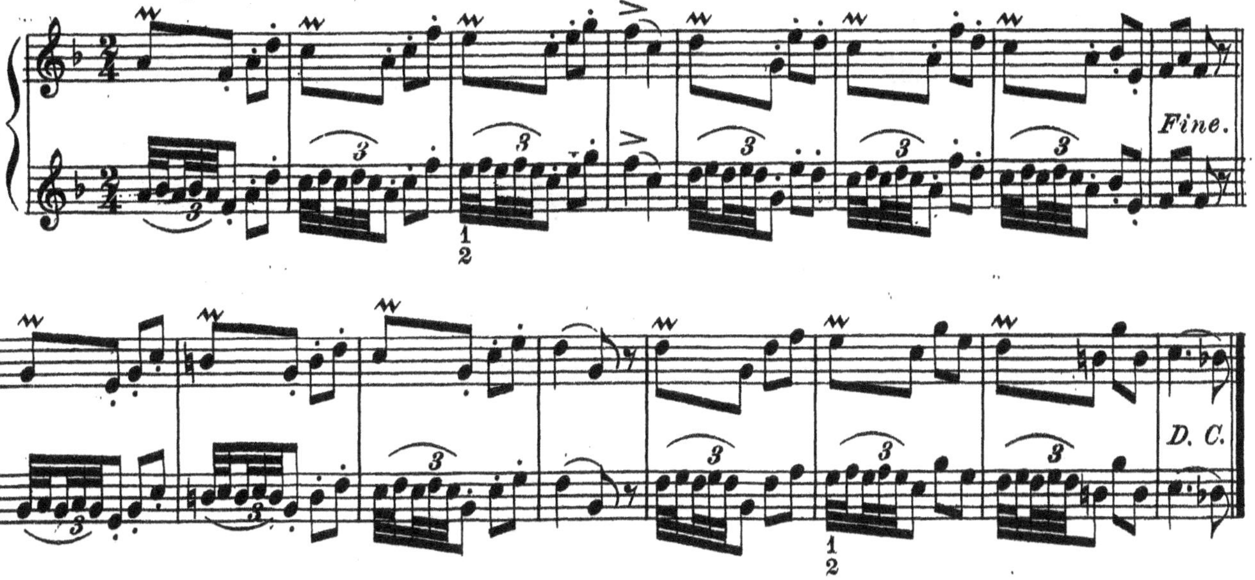

Allegro.

84.

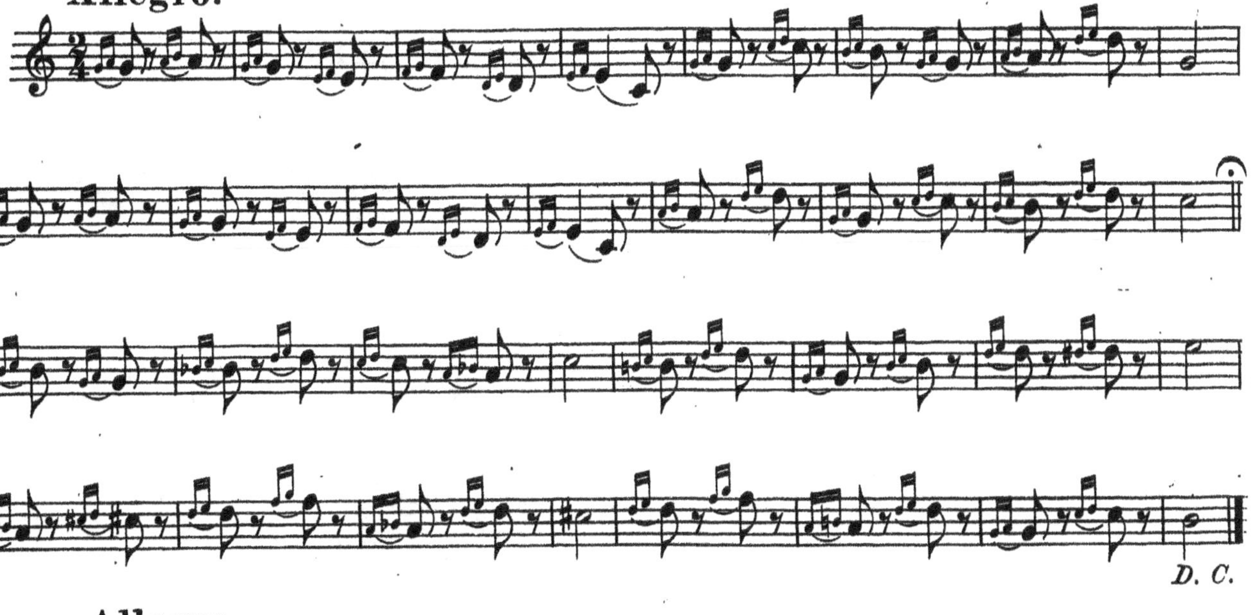

Allegro.

85.

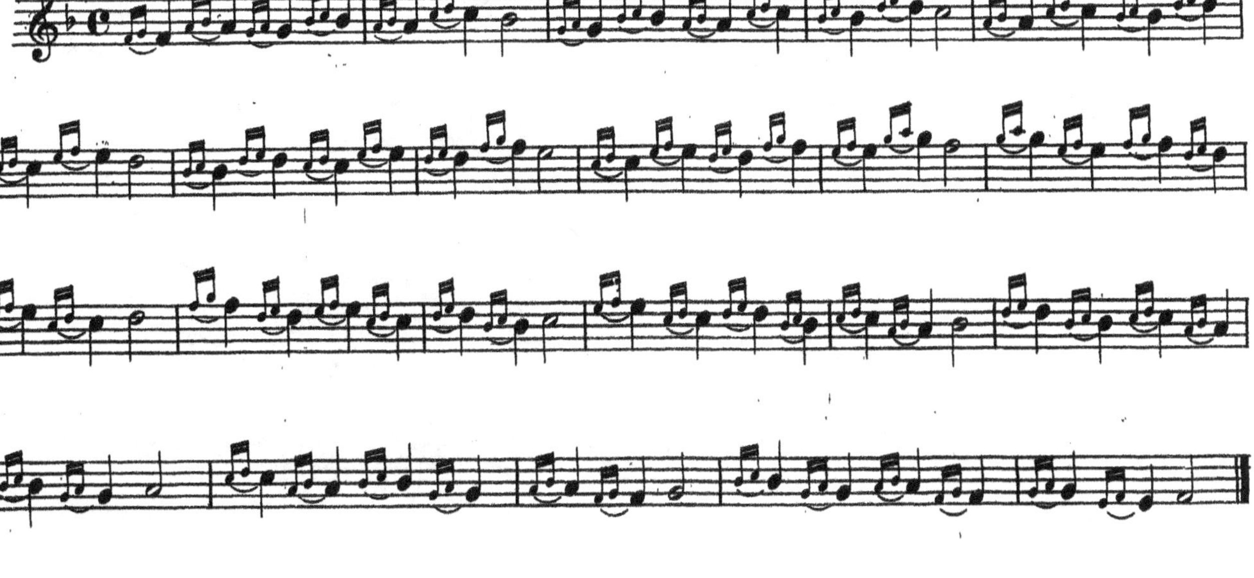

Intervals.

Exercises for the intervals should be practiced assiduously, and care is to be taken not to alter the position of the mouthpiece when passing from a low to a high, or a high to a low one. By observing this rule, the player will acquire certainty in taking the notes and great facility in their execution. (See from No. 1 to 7.)

Octaves and Tenths.

Octaves and Tenths are not used to any extent on the cornet; however, considerable effect may be produced by a judicious use of octaves.

As to tenths, they may be classed under the preceding category. It would indeed be very difficult to execute with rapidity any melody whatsoever, if the interval of the tenth were consecutively employed. (See from No. 8 to 12.)

Triplets.

The use of triplets is always highly effective. In order to execute a triplet well, each note must be uttered with perfect equality. The student should proceed slowly at first, and not attempt to play quickly until the fingers have acquired regularity of motion. (See from No. 13 to 27.)

Studies in Sixteenth notes.

In order to arrive at perfection of execution, these studies should be played with scrupulous attention to time and rhythm, and due regard to the articulations therein indicated. The performer should begin slowly and increase his speed until he has become familiar with the exercise. Too great a rapidity of execution does not always impart to the performance the brilliancy expected. Precision and regularity are the real foundation of an excellent execution. (See from No. 28 to 47.)

The Perfect Major and Minor Chord.

In providing so many of these studies, my motive has been to enable the pupil, by degrees, to play with ease in every key. Some of the fingerings may at first appear difficult, but this is no reason for setting them aside; on the contrary, it should serve as a motive for working at them with courage and resolution. Some benefit must always result from labor of this kind, even if the notes be executed slowly; and the efforts made to overcome certain "impossibilities" will soon prove that they were only impossible in appearance. (See from No. 48 to 52.)

Von den Intervallsprüngen.

Es ist gut, diese Art von Etuden eifrig zu üben, und dabei Sorge zu tragen, dass das Mundstück auf den Lippen nicht versetzt wird, wenn man von einer tiefen zu einer hohen oder von einer hohen zu einer tiefen Note übergehen will. Man erlangt dadurch eine grosse Sicherheit des Ansatzes und Leichtigkeit der Ausführung. (Siehe No.1 bis 7)

Von den Octaven und Decimen.

Die Octaven und decimen sind auf dem Cornet à pistons nicht sehr gebräuchlich; nichtsdestoweniger kann man durch eine verständige Anwendung der Octaven eine gute Wirkung hervorbringen.

Was die Decimen anbetrifft, so kann man sie unter die Intervallsprünge rechnen, indessen würde es sehr schwierig sein, mit Schnelligkeit irgend eine Melodie anzuführen und dabei hintereinander das Decimenintervall anwenden zu wollen. (Siehe No.8 bis 12.)

Von den Triolen.

Die Anwendung der Triolen ist immer von ausgezeichneter Wirkung. Um die Triole gut auszuführen, muss man sich üben, jede Note mit vollkommener Gleichmässigkeit anzugeben. Man muss anfangs langsam üben, und erst zu einer lebhafteren Bewegung übergehen, wenn die Fingerbewegung eine vollkommen regelmässige ist. (Siehe No. 13 bis No. 27.)

Von den Sechszehnteln.

Um zu einer untadligen Ausführung zu gelangen, muss man diese Etuden streng im Tacte üben und die vorgeschriebenen Accente genau beachten. Man muss langsam anfangen und das Tempo in dem Maasse beschleunigen, als man sich mit der Uebung nach und nach vertraut macht. Zu grosse Schnelligkeit giebt der Ausführung nicht immer den Glanz, den man erwartet. Die wahren Kennzeichen einer guten Ausführung sind Sauberkeit und Regelmässigkeit. (Siehe No. 28 bis No. 47.)

Vom Dur- und Moll-Accord.

Indem ich diesen Etuden eine grosse Ausdehnung verlieh, war es meine Absicht, die Schüler dahin zu führen, dass sie sich in allen Tonarten mit Leichtigkeit bewegen können. Einige Fingersätze werden anfänglich schwer erscheinen. Dies ist jedoch kein Grund, sie bei Seite zu lassen, sondern man soll sie mit desto mehr Muth und Festigkeit angreifen. Diese Accorde bleiben immer schwierig, selbst wenn man sie langsam ausführt; aber die Mühe die man sich giebt, um gewisse Unmöglichkeiten zu besiegen, wird bald lehren, dass sie nur scheinbar waren. Nur diejenigen Künstler werden unübersteigliche Schwierigkeiten darin finden, die überhaupt aus Bequemlichkeit die traurige Gewohnheit haben, stets nur in leichten Tonarten zu blasen. (Siehe No. 48 bis No. 52.)

Des sauts d'intervalles.

Il convient de travailler avec assiduité ce genre d'études, en ayant bien soin de ne pas deranger l'embouchure de dessus les lèvres, pour passer d'une note basse à une note haute, ou d'une note haute à une note basse. On obtient par là une grande sûreté d'attaque et une grande facilité d'exécution. (Voyez du no. 1 au no. 7.)

Des Octaves et des Dixièmes.

Les octaves et les dixièmes ne sont pas trèsusités sur le cornet à pistons; on peut néanmoins produire beaucoup d'effet par un intelligent emploi des octaves.

Quant aux dixièmes, il y a lieu de les ranger parmi les sauts d'intervalles. Il serait fort difficile, en effet d'exécuter avec vitesse une mélodie quelconque, en employant successivement l'intervalle de dixième. (Voyez du no. 8 au no. 12.)

Des Triolets.

L'emploi des triolets a toujours été d'un excellent effet. Pour bien rendre le triolet, il faut s'etudier à faire parler chaque note avec une parfaite égalité. On doit travailler d'abord lentement, et ne passer a un mouvement plus vif que lorsque les doigts marchent avec régularité. (Voyez du no. 13 au no. 27.)

Etudes en doubles croches.

Pour arriver à une exécution irréprochable, on doit travailler ces études en conservant toujours une mesure bien rhythmée, et en suivant ponctuellement les articulations qui sont indiquées. Il faut débuter avec lenteur et ne presser le mouvement qu'au fur et a mesure qu'on se familiarise avec l'exercice. Une trop grande vitesse ne donne pas toujours au jeu le brillant qu'on espère. La netteté et la régularité, voilà les vrais types d'une belle exécution. (Voyez du no. 28 au no. 47.)

De l'accord parfait majeur et mineur.

En donnant un aussi grand developpement à ces études, mon intention a été d'amener les élèves à pouvoir jouer aisément dans tous les tons. Certains doigtés paraîtront au premier abord difficiles; ce n'est pas une raison pour les laisser de côté, c'en est une, au contraire, pour les aborder avec courage et conviction. Il reste toujours quelque chose d'un pareil travail, même si on exécute lentement ces accords; et les efforts que l'on aura faits pour vaincre certaines impossibilités montreront bien vite qu'elles ne sont qu'apparentes. Elles n'offriront d'obstacle insurmontable qu'aux artistes qui, par paresse, auront contracté la funeste habitude de jouer toujours dans des tons simples. (Voyez du no. 48 au no. 52.)

The Chord of the Dominant Seventh.

The chord of the dominant seventh is the same in both the major and minor keys. Here it becomes the complement of the preceding studies. When practicing it, the regularity which I have already enjoined and which I cannot too strenuously recommend, should carefully be observed. (See Nos. 53 and 54.)

The Chord of the Diminished Seventh.

This chord plays a conspicuous part in modern musical composition. Owing to its elastic nature, it is of incalculable service; for, consisting as it does solely of minor thirds, it may be interpreted in various different ways, and there are innumerable cases in which the musician may have recourse to it.

Nevertheless, it occupies a regular place in the minor scale, as may be seen from study No. 55, in which its real place has been assigned to it.

Successive chords of diminished sevenths are admissible, inasmuch as they follow one another with considerable facility. I have presented this chord in various rhythms and combinations, in order that the pupil may be fully enabled to judge of its effect. (See from No. 55 to 61.)

The Cadence.

I am adding a series of cadences in form of preludes to these studies, in order to accustom the pupil to terminate a solo effectively. It is also advisable to transpose these cadences to all the different keys. Care must be taken to breathe whenever a rest occurs, so as to reach the end of the phrase with full power, and in perfect tune; otherwise the effect will be completely destroyed.

Vom Dominant-Septimen-Accord.

Der Dominant-Septimen-Accord, welcher in den Dur-und Molltonarten stets derselbe ist, dient hier zur Vervollständigung der vorhergehenden Uebungen. Bei seiner Uebung bewahre man stets diejenige Regelmässigkeit, welche ich nicht zu sehr einschärfen kann. (Siehe No. 53 und No. 54.)

Vom verminderten Septimen-Accord.

Dieser Accord spielt eine grosse Rolle in der Musik der Gegenwart. Dank seiner Elasticität, leistet er der Modulation unberechenbare Dienste. Ausschliesslich aus kleiner Terzen gebildet, kann man ihn auf sehr verschiedene Weise auflösen und es giebt eine Menge von Fällen, in welchen der Musiker sich seiner bedient.

Er nimmt indessen auch eine regelmässige Stelle in der Molltonleiter ein, wei man aus der Uebung No. 55 ersehen kann, worin ich ihm seine wahre Stellung angewiesen habe.

Man kann mehrere verminderte Septimen-Accorde auf einander folgen lassen, vorausgesetzt dass sie sich mit grosser Leichtigkeit an einander anschliessen. Ich gebe den Accord in verschiedenen Rhythmen und Verbindungen, damit der Schüler sich von seiner Wirkung wohl überzeuge. (Siehe No. 55 bis 61.)

Von den Cadenzen.

Ich füge diesen Etuden eine Reihe von Cadenzen in Form von Präludien hinzu, um den Schüler an einen guten Abschluss des Solos zu gewöhnen. Man wird wohl thun, diese Cadenzen in allen Tonarten zu transponiren. Man muss Sorge tragen, an denjenigen Stellen, wo sich Pausen befinden, wohl Athem zu schöpfen, damit man die Phrasen mit Kraft und ohne den Ton sinken zu lassen, schliessen kann. Andernfalls würde die Wirkung vollständig vernichtet.

De l'accord de septième dominante.

L'accord de septième dominante étant le même dans les modes majeur et mineur, devient ici le complément des études précédentes. On devra le travailler en conservant toujours cette même régularité que je ne saurais trop recommander. (Voyez les nos. 53 et 54.)

De l'accord de septième diminuée.

Cet accord joue une grand rôle dans la composition musicale actuelle; il rend, grâce à son élasticité, des services incalculables; car, uniquement composé de tierces mineures, on peut l'interpréter de bien des manières différentes, et il y a une foule de cas où le musicien y a recours.

Il occupe cependant une place régulière dans la gamme mineure, ainsi que l'on en pourra juger par l'étude no. 55, dans laquelle je lui ai assigné son véritable rang.

On peut faire des successions d'accords de septièmes diminuées, attendu qu'ils s'enchaînent avec beaucoup de facilité. J'ai présenté cet accord dans des rhythmes et dans des enchaînements différents, afin que l'élève puisse se rendre bien compte de son effet. (Voyez du no. 55 au no. 61.)

Du point d'orgue.

Je joins à ces études une série de points d'orgue en forme de préludes, afin d'habituer les élèves à bien terminer un solo. Il sera bien de transporter ces points d'orgue dans tous les tons. Il faut avoir soin de respirer aux endroits où se recontrent des repos, afin d'arriver à la conclusion de la phrase avec toute sa force, et sans laisser tomber le son; autrement l'effet se trouverait complètement annihilé.

STUDIES ON THE INTERVALS.
STUDIEN ÜBER DIE INTERVALLE.
ETUDES SUR LES INTERVALLES.

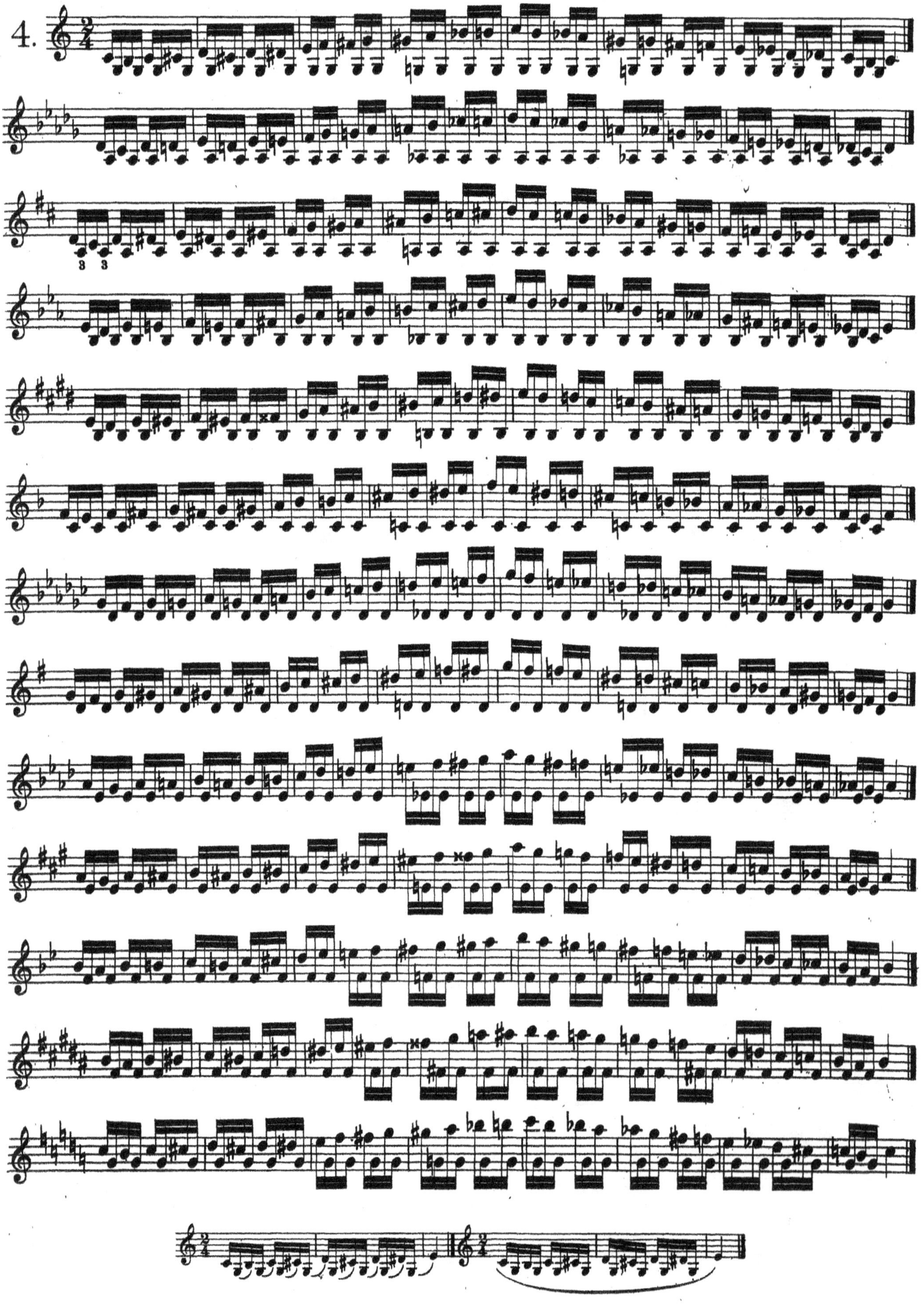
4.

130

OCTAVES AND TENTHS.   VON DEN OCTAVEN UND DECIMEN.   DES OCTAVES ET DES DIXIÈMES.

132

EXERCISES ON TRIPLETS. **STUDIEN ÜBER DIE TRIOLEN.** **ETUDES SUR LES TRIOLETS.**

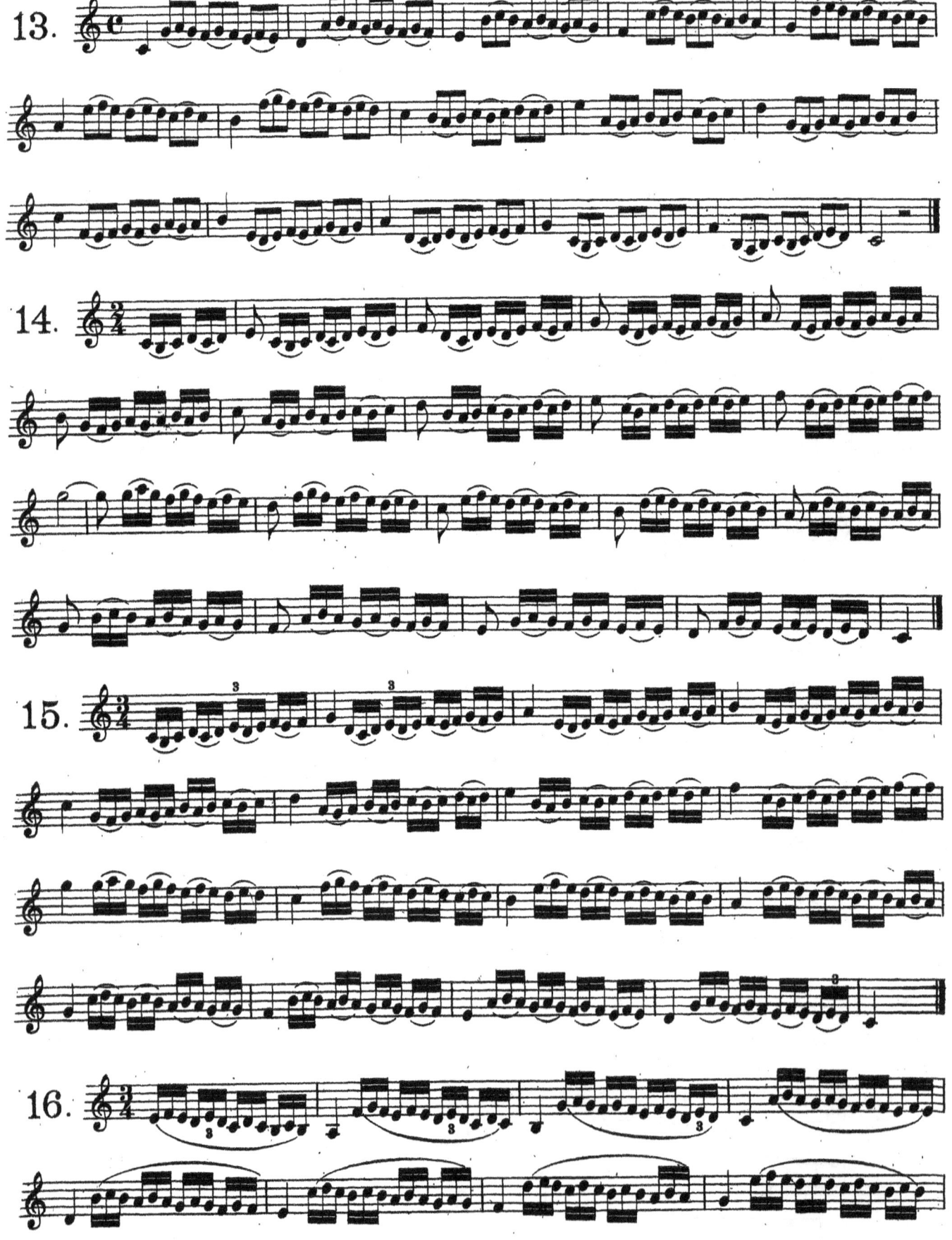

EXERCISES ON SIXTEENTH NOTES. / STUDIEN IN SECHZEHNTELN. / ÉTUDES EN DOUBLES CROCHES.

MAJOR AND MINOR CHORDS.
VOM DUR UND MOLL ACCORD.
DE L'ACCORD PARFAIT MAJOR ET MINEUR.

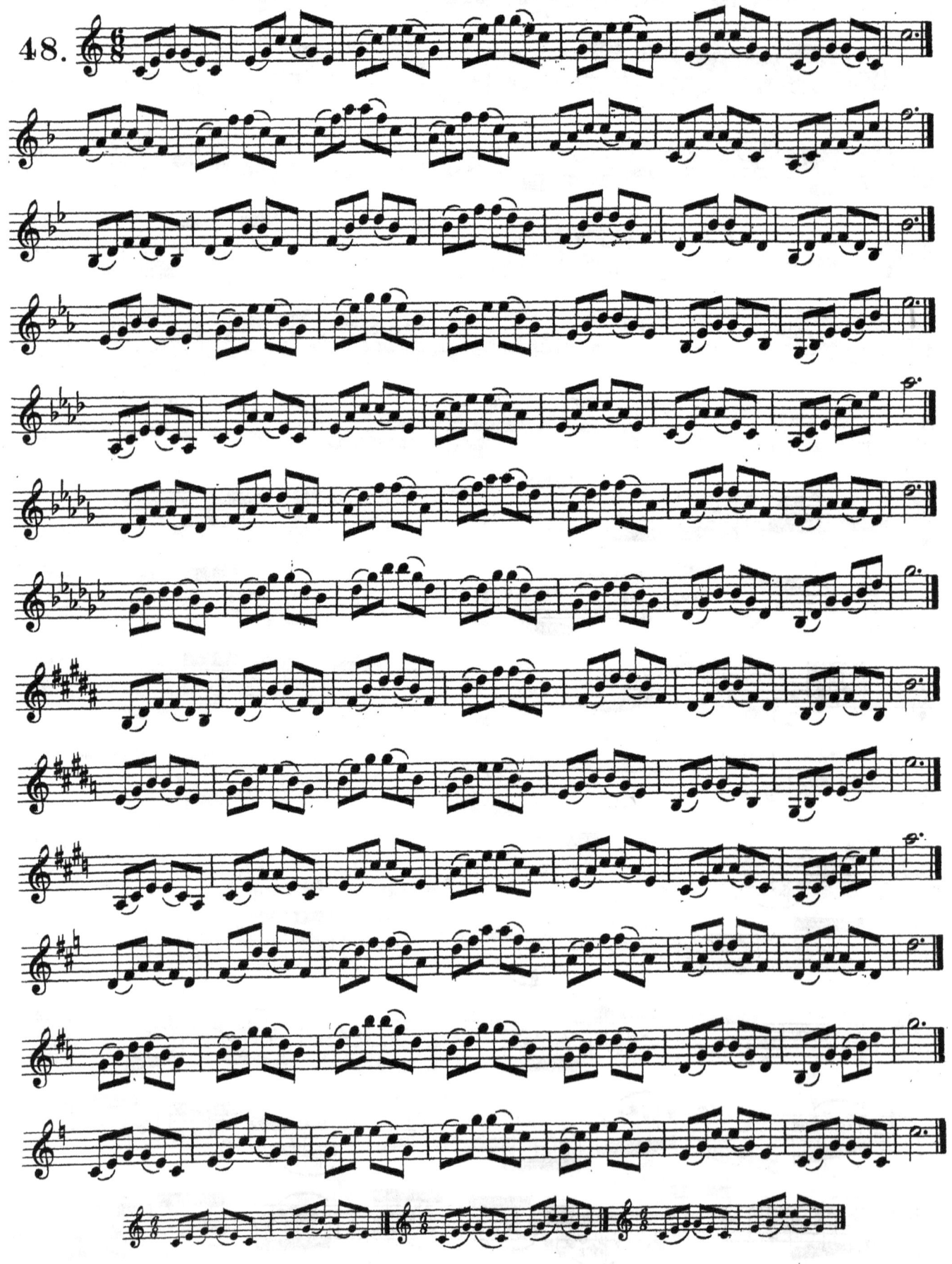

48.

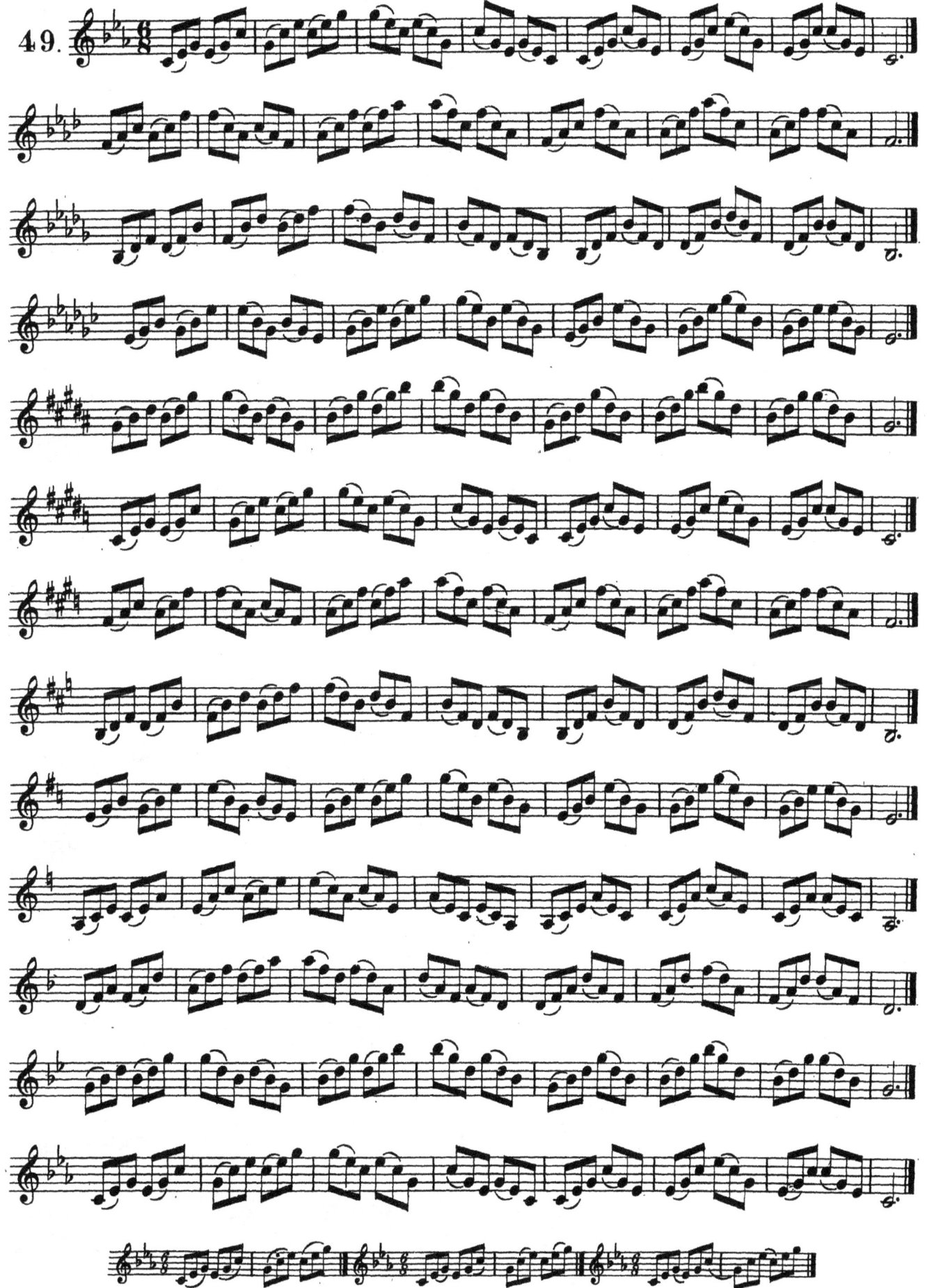

144

50.

THE CHORD OF THE DOMINANT SEVENTH.
VOM DOMINANT SEPTIMEN-ACCORD.
DE L'ACCORD DU SEPTIÈME DOMINANTE.

148

54.

THE CHORD OF THE DIMINISHED SEVENTH.
VOM VERMINDERTEN SEPTIMEN ACCORD.
DE L'ACCORD SEPTIÈME DIMINUÉE.

150

152

CADENCES. | *CADENZEN.* | POINTS D'ORGUE.

62.

DESCRIPTIVE ADVICE on Tonguing.

Triple Tonguing.

The staccato consists in detaching a succession of notes with regularity, without allowing the tonguing to be either too short, or too long. In order to arrive at this degree of perfection the earlier studies, which serve as the basis, should be very slowly practiced.

The student should first strive to pronounce, with perfect equality, the syllables:

tu tu ku tu tu ku tu tu ku tu tu ku tu

In order to impart more equality to the tonguing, it is necessary, when beginning, to prolong each syllable a little. When great precision has been obtained in the utterance of the tonguing, it should then be more briefly emitted, in order to obtain the true staccato.

I will now describe the mechanism of the triple staccato.

In pronouncing the syllables tu tu, the tongue places itself against the teeth of the upper jaw, and in retiring pronounces the first two sounds. The tongue should then reascend to the roof of the mouth and obstruct the throat, dilating itself by the effect of the pronunciation of the syllable ku, which, by allowing a column of air to penetrate into the mouthpiece, determines the third sound.

In order to invest this to-and-fro motion with perfect regularity, it is necessary to practice slowly, so that the tongue, like a valve, may allow the same quantity of air to escape at each syllable.

If this system of articulation is persevered in, no passage will be found difficult; the tone-production on the cornet will be as easy as that on the flute; but to reach this end, the pronunciation must be perfectly pure. Experience has proven to me that to obtain a really irreproachable execution, it is necessary to pronounce the syllables tu tu ku tu tu ku tu, as has just been shown, and not the syllables du du gu du du gu du. These latter, it is true, go faster, but do not sufficiently detail the sound.

The tonguing should not be too precipitated, for the auditor will then be no longer able to distinguish it. A sufficient degree of rapidity may be obtained by the method I have indicated. The most important points to master are clearness and precision. (No. 1 to No. 76.)

Double Tonguing.

This kind of staccato is of great assistance in the execution of scales, or arpeg-

ERKLÄRUNGEN über den Zungenstoss.

Vom Zungenstoss beim dreifachen Staccato.

Das Staccato besteht darin, eine Reihe von Tönen in gleichartiger Weise abzustossen, ohne dass der Zungenstoss zu kurz, noch zu lang ist. Um zu dieser Vollkommenheit zu gelangen übe man die ersten Etuden, die als Anfangspunkt dienen, sehr langsam.

Zuerst bemühe man sich, die folgenden Sylben mit grösster Gleichmässigkeit auszusprechen:

Um dem Zungenstoss mehr Gleichmässigkeit zu geben, verlängere man anfänglich die Sylben ein wenig, so dass die Töne sich wohl untereinander binden. Erst, wenn der Zungenstoss mit Präcision gelingt, darf man ihn etwas kürzer machen, um das wirkliche Staccato zu erhalten.

Der Mechanismus des dreifachen Staccato ist folgender:

Indem man die Sylben tü tü ausspricht, legt man die Zunge gegen die oberen Zähne, und indem man sie zurückzieht, bringt man die beiden ersten Stösse hervor. Die Zunge muss sich hierauf nach dem hinteren Theil des Mundes zurückziehen, und die Kehle schliessen, indem sie sich zur Bildung der Sylbe kü aufbäumt, die dann, indem die Luft in das Mundstück eindringt, den dritten Stoss hervorbringt.

Damit dieses Hin- und Hergehen mit grosser Regelmässigkeit geschehe, muss man es sehr langsam üben, so dass die Zunge, gleich wie ein Ventil, bei jeder Sylbe eine gleiche Luftmenge entweichen lässt.

Dank dieser Art der Articulation, giebt es keine Schwierigkeiten mehr. Man gelangt dahin, das Cornet so leicht zu blasen, wie die Flöte. Dazu ist jedoch eine vollkommen reine Aussprache nöthig. Die Erfahrung hat mich gelehrt, dass man, um ein vollkommen perlendes Staccato zu bekommen, die Sylben tü tü kü tü tü kü tü genau, wie es vorgeschrieben, aussprechen muss, und nicht die Sylben dü dü gü dü dü gü dü. Die letzteren gehen allerdings schneller zu prononciren, aber statt die Töne zu sondern, bringen sie einen Zungendruck in dem Tone hervor.

Der Zungenstoss darf nicht übereilt werden, da ihn der Hörer dann zuletzt nicht mehr unterscheidet. Man erinnere sich wohl, dass diese Articulation dazu dienen soll, Gänge auszuführen, in denen bei jedem Zungenstoss auch der Ton wechselt, nicht aber das Geräusch einer Karre nachzuahmen. Man erlangt übrigens durch das Mittel, welches ich angegeben, eine durchaus hinreichende Schnelligkeit. Wonach man hauptsächlich streben muss, ist die Erlangung einer untadelhaften Präcision und Sauberkeit. (Siehe No. 1 bis No. 76.)

Vom Zungenstoss im zweitheiligen Staccato.

Diese Art des Staccato ist von grossem Nutzen für die Ausführung von Tonleitern,

EXPLICATIONS sur le coup de langue.

Du coup de langue en staccato ternaire.

Le staccato consiste à détacher avec régularité une succession de notes, sans que le coup de langue soit ni trop sec, ni trop allongé. Pour arriver à une telle perfection, on devra travailler très-lentement les premières études qui servent de point de départ.

Il faut primitivement s'appliquer à prononcer avec beaucoup d'égalité les syllabes:

Pour donner plus d'égalité au coup de langue, il faut, en commençant, allonger un peu chaque syllabe, de manière à bien lier les notes entre elles. Ce n'est que lorsque le coup de langue sort avec précison que l'on doit prononcer avec plus de sécheresse, afin d'obtenir le vrai staccato.

Voici le mécanisme du staccato ternaire.

En prononçant les syllabes tu tu, la langue se place contre les dents de la mâchoire supérieure et, en se retirant, produit les deux premiers coups. La langue doit alors remonter au fond de la bouche et obstruer le gosier en se gonflant par l'effet de la prononciation de la syllabe ku, qui, en laissant pénétrer la colonne d'air dans l'embouchure, détermine le troisième coup.

Pour donner à cet effet de va-et-vient une grande régularité, il faut travailler lentement afin que la langue, tout comme le ferait une soupape, laisse échapper à chaque syllabe la même quantité d'air.

Grâce à ce genre d'articulation, il n'y a plus de traits difficiles; on peut arriver à jouer aussi facilement que le fait la flûte; mais il faut, pour cela, une prononciation d'une grande pureté. L'expérience m'a démontré que pour obtenir un staccato vraiment perlé, il faut prononcer les syllabes tu tu ku tu tu ku tu, comme il vient d'être indiqué, et non pas les syllabes du du gu du du gu du; ces dernières vont plus vite, il est vrai; mais, au lieu de détacher, elles produisent un coup de langue dans le son.

Le coup de langue ne doit pas être trop précipité, car alors l'auditeur finit par ne plus le distinguer. Il faut bien se rappeler que cette articulation doit servir à exécuter des traits en changeant de note sur chaque coup de langue, et non pas à imiter le bruit de la crécelle. On obtient, au reste, une très-suffisante vitesse par le moyen que j'ai indiqué. Ce à quoi il faut principalement s'appliquer, c'est à réaliser une précison et une netteté irréprochables. (Voyez du no. 1 au no. 76.)

Du coup de langue en staccato binaire.

Ce genre de staccato est d'un grand secours dans l'exécution des gammes, des ar-

gios, in the binary rhythm. In order to execute this exercise with precision, it must be practiced slowly, always having regard for the principles set forth for triple tonguing.

First of all, the student should pronounce the syllables:

tu ku tu ku tu ku tu ku tu

As is seen, the tongue performs a to-and-fro movement, which it is very difficult to obtain with perfect equality; but once this has been attained, the most difficult passages may be executed with all desirable speed, energy, and strength.

After having practiced all the studies connected with this kind of articulation, recourse may then be had to the scales, the perfect chords, the chords of the dominant seventh and diminished seventh. These should be executed by employing the same staccato, so as to accustom the fingers to proceed in conformity with the tongue. This practice will be fruitful in its results. (See from No. 77 to 114.)

The Slur in Double Tonguing.

In order to combine slurs with the double staccato, a peculiar kind of pronunciation must be employed. It would be monotonous to employ staccatos continually without having occasional reference to the slur. The combination of the two occasions a pleasing variety in execution, at the same time facilitating the acceleration of the movement.

This articulation is obtained by pronouncing the following syllables:

ta-a taka ta-a taka   ta-a taka taka ta-ka   ta-a taka ta-a taka   ta-a taka taka taka ta

The syllable 'a serves to strike the first note, and the syllable a, which comes afterwards, enables the performer, by prolonging the sound, to slur easily to the second note. This tonguing is assuredly one of the most indispensable, inasmuch as it is to be met with in all kinds of music. (See No. 114 to 134.)

Tonguing as applied to the Trumpet.

Having frequently observed that many pupils, both at the Conservatory and elsewhere, who were able to perform the trumpet tonguing, scarcely ever succeeded in correctly performing the true staccato, I conclude therefrom that this tonguing is an obstacle to the other articulations, and I therefore recommend students not to practice this, until they shall have thoroughly mastered all the others. Moreover, its execution is extremely easy, when the student is really capable of performing the double and triple tonguing. (See No. 135 to No. 145.)

TRIPLE TONGUING.
VOM ZUNGENSTOSS BEIM DREIFACHEN STACCATO.
DU COUP DE LANGUE EN STACCATO TERNAIRE.

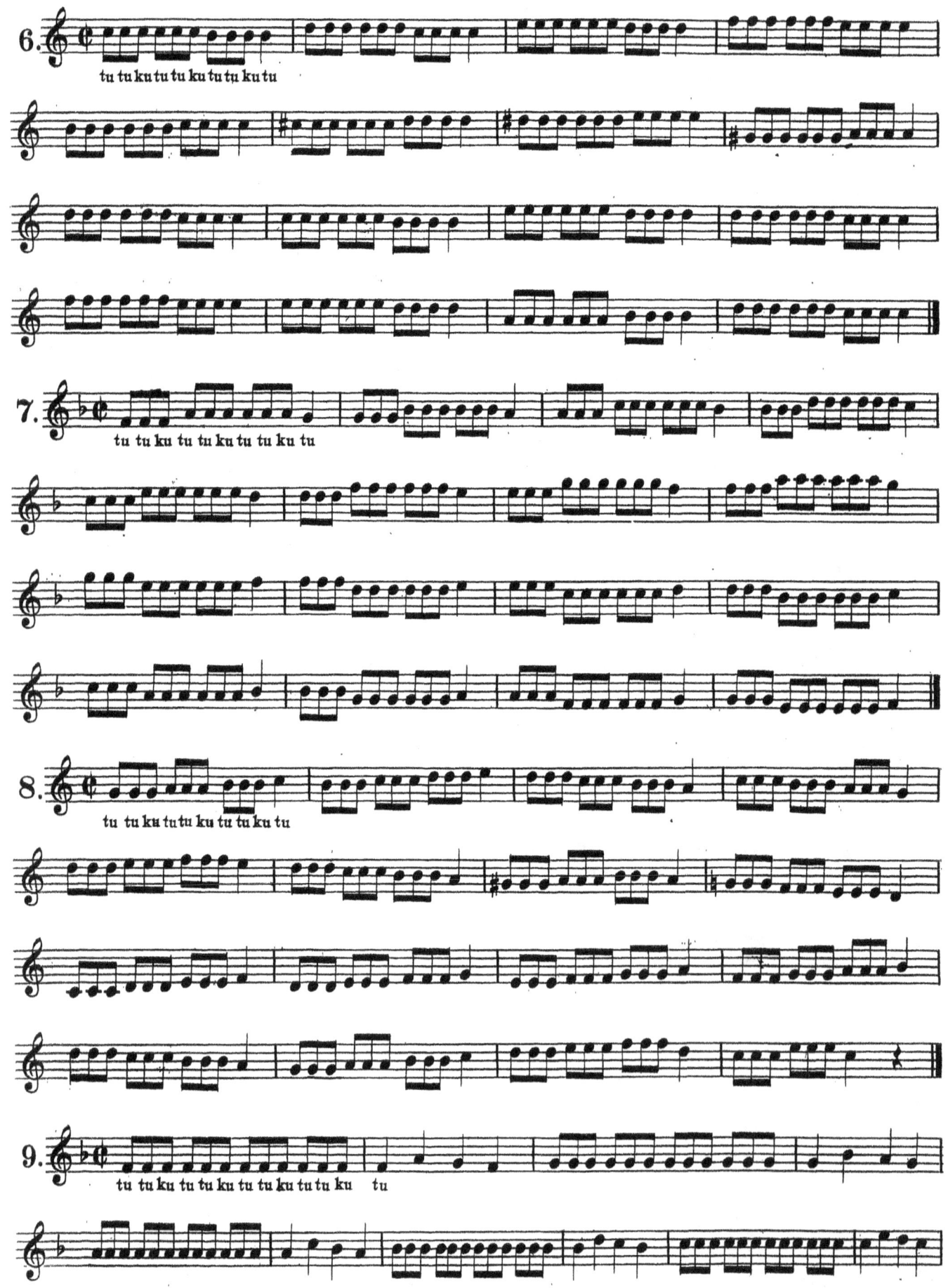

164

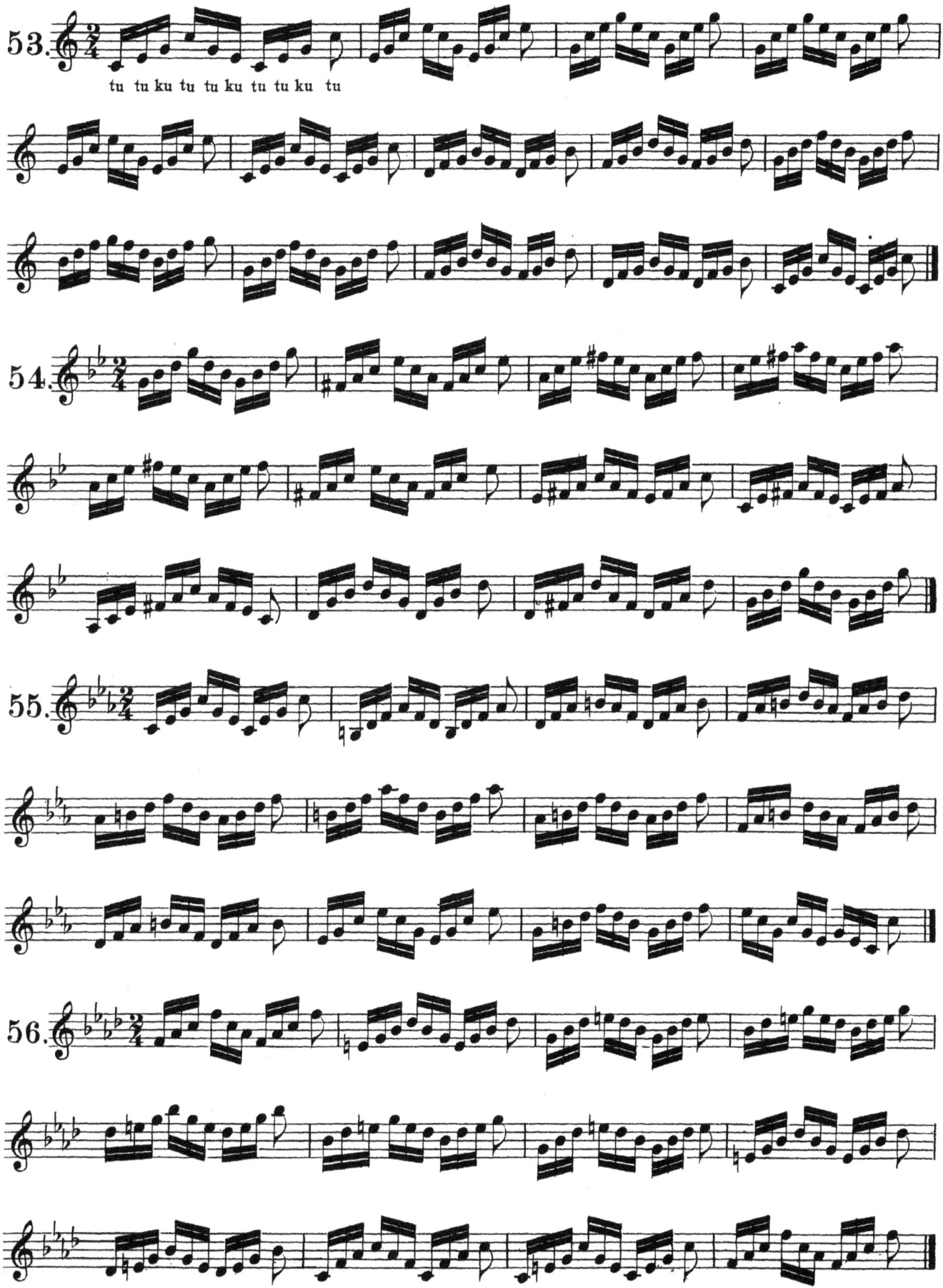

172

DOUBLE TONGUING.
VOM ZUNGENSTOSS BEIM ZWEIFACHEN STACCATO.
DU COUP DE LANGUE EN STACCATO BINAIRE.

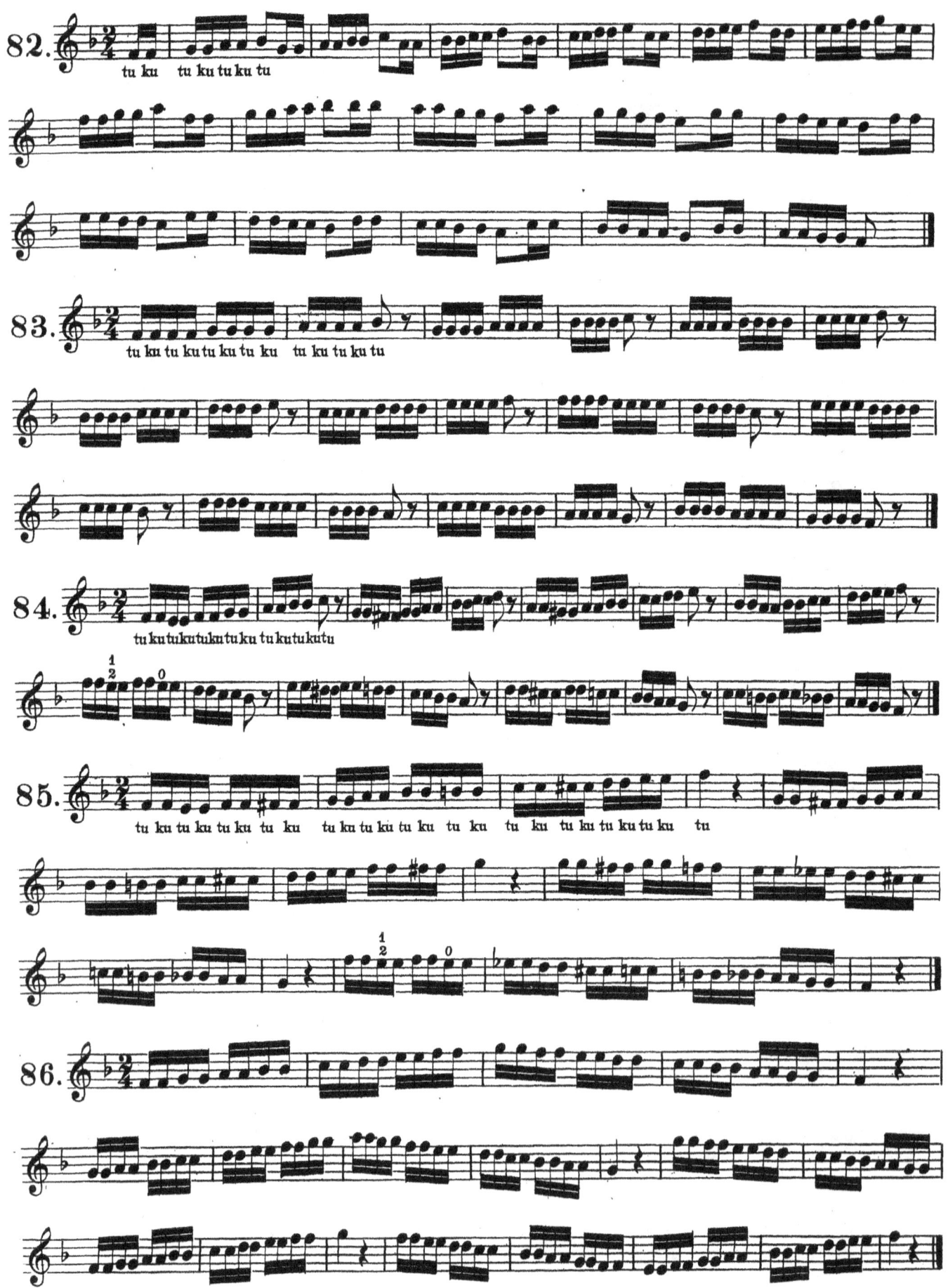

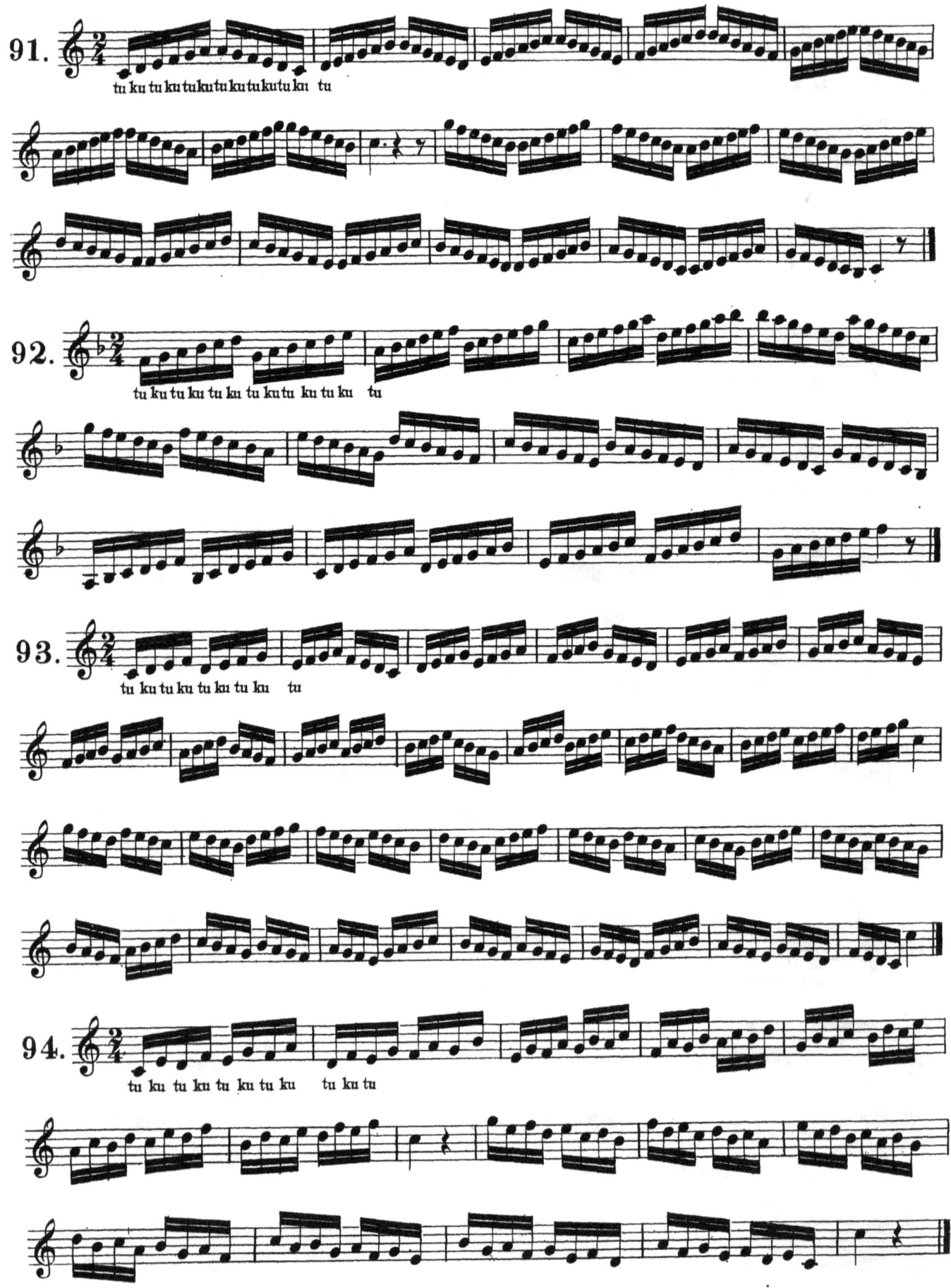

THE SLUR AND DOUBLE TONGUING.
VOM SCHLEIFEN BEIM ZWEIFACHEN STACCATO.
DU COULÉ DANS LE STACCATO BINAIRE.

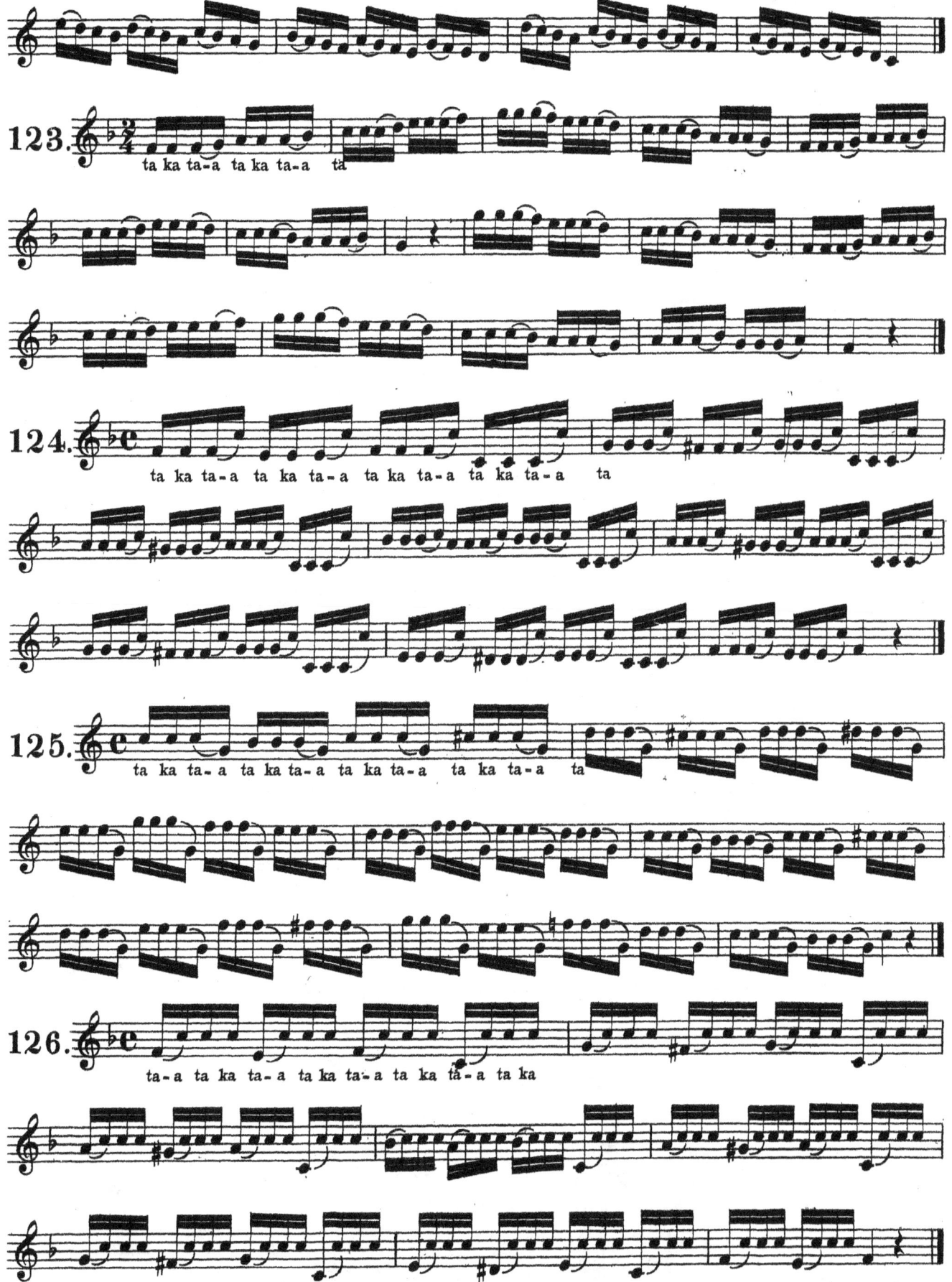

TONGUING AS APPLIED TO THE TRUMPET.
VOM ZUNGENSTOSS BEI DER TROMPETE.
DU COUP DE LANGUE DE TROMPETTE.

THE ART OF PHRASING.
150 CLASSIC AND POPULAR MELODIES.

Arranged by Arban. *(Professor of the Imperial Conservatory of Music.)*

ROBIN ADAIR.

LOVING, I THINK OF THEE.

Krebs.

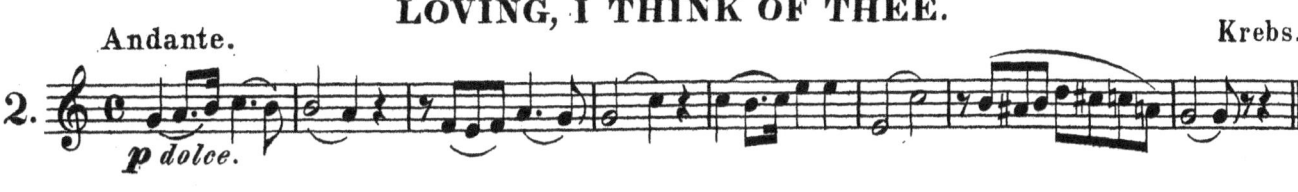

MY PRETTY JANE.

199

MY BARK WHICH O'ER THE TIDE.

31. Allegretto. — Balfe.

'TWAS RANK AND FAME.

32. And.te cantabile. — Balfe.

VIEN, LEONORA.

33. Larghetto. — Donizetti.

205

THE EXILE'S LAMENT.

Rich. Albert.

52.

SICILIAN VESPERS.

Verdi.

53.

I THINK OF THEE.

F. Abt.

54.

LA CENERENTOLA.
Rossini.

61. Moderato.

QUANDO LE SERE AL PLACIDO.
Verdi.

62. Andante.

ALLA VITA CHE T'ARRIDE.
Verdi.

63. Andante.

Presto.

Cad. ad lib.

209

THE IRISH EMIGRANT.

G. Barker.

DON JUAN.

Mozart.

CAN I BE DREAMING?
from "The Talisman."

Balfe.

LE DESIR.

Beethoven.

ANDANTE FROM A MAJOR SYMPHONY.

Mendelssohn.

AL BEN DE' TUOI QUAL VITTIMA.

216

ORANGE AND BLUE JIG.

LANCASHIRE CLOG DANCE.

IL TROVATORE. — Verdi.

THE MAGIC FLUTE. — Mozart.

AUSTRIAN HYMN.

127. Maestoso.

LA SOMNAMBULE.
Bellini.

128. Allegro.

LA PARISINA ROMANZA.
Donizetti.

129. Moderato.

IN MIA MAN ALFIN TU SEI.

IL RIVAL SALVAR TU DEI.

THOU ART SO NEAR, AND YET SO FAR.

Reichardt.

WHEN THE QUIET MOON IS BEAMING.

Schondorf.

236

STAR OF PARIS POLKA.

142.

CAVATINA FROM "ERNANI."

Verdi.

THE PILGRIM OF LOVE.

"DEAR LITTLE HEART."

"HOME SWEET HOME."

"KEEL ROW."

241

242

"BLUE BELLS OF SCOTLAND."

GOD SAVE THE QUEEN.
America.

150.

Sixty-eight Duets for TWO CORNETS.

249

"AIR BY GRETRY."

"NOEL ANCIEN."

250

"AIR BY BEETHOVEN."

"ARABIAN SONG."

252

"ROMANCE."

Andte sostenuto.   De Gouy.

17.

"NOEL ANCIEN."

"MARCH."

De Gouy.

"THE TWO SAVOYARDS."

"SILENT SORROW."
Webbe.

"MELODY."

"THE LION HUNT."

Allegretto.   Saverio.

"L'ELISIRE D'AMORE."

Donizetti.

"I WOULD THAT MY LOVE."

Mendelssohn.

"PRAYER TO THE VIRGIN."

Saverio.

All⁰ moderato.

29.

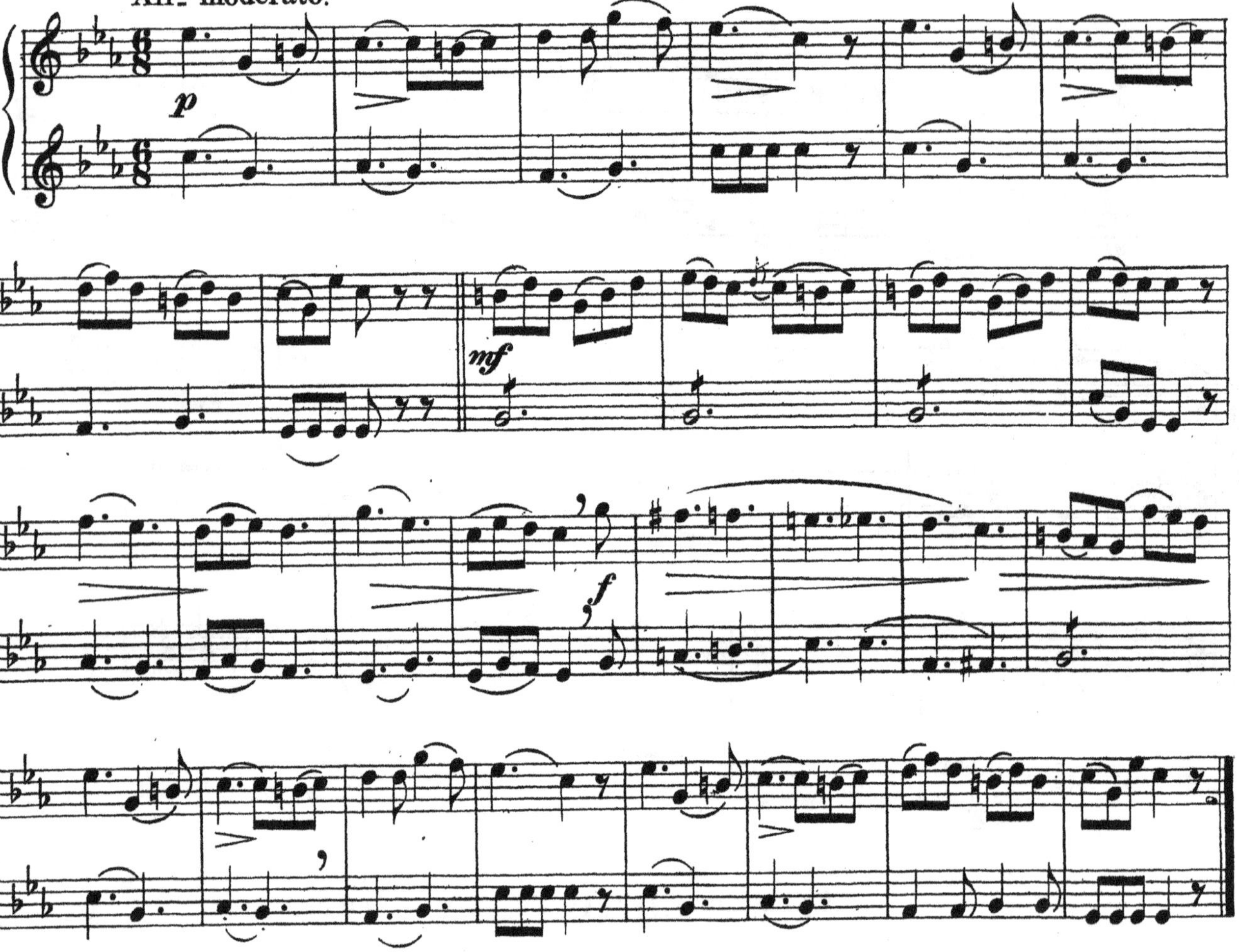

"SPANISH ROYAL MARCH."

30.

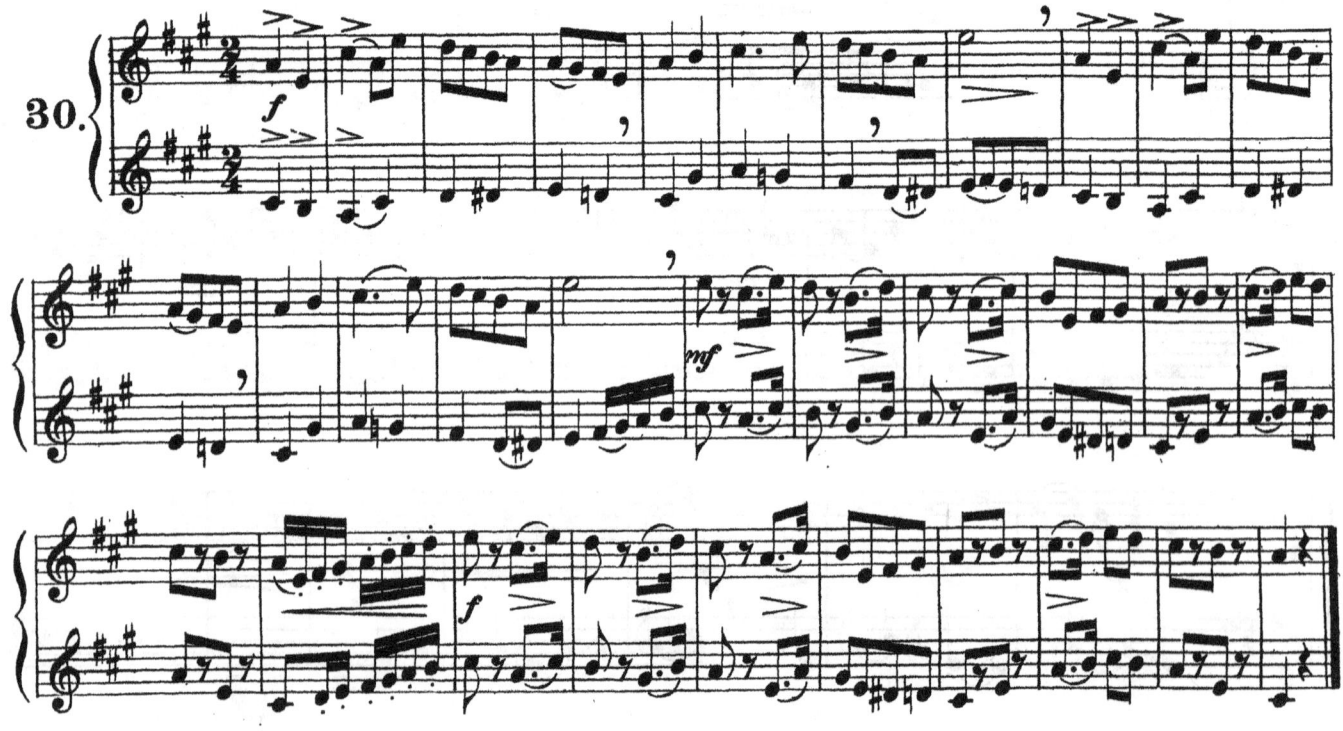

"MARCH OF TWO MISERS."

"MELODY."

"COUNTRY WEDDING."

"BIVOUAC SONG."

261

"BIRTHDAY FESTIVAL."

"MELODY."

"GERMAN SONG."
Kücken.

264

"BOLERO."

Lightly.　　　　　　　　　　　　　　　　　　　　　　　　　　　　De Gouy.

43.

CAVATINA FROM "SOMNAMBULA."

Bellini.

"AUSTRIAN NATIONAL HYMN."

Haydn.

"FREISCHÜTZ." Weber.

FRENCH AIR.

AIR FROM "SOMNAMBULA."

Bellini.

"WIND AND WAVE."

"TYROLIENNE."

"ITALIAN AIR."

272

"ALPINE HORN."

58. Andante. *mf con espressione.* — Proch.

Fine. *f* *cresc.* D.S.

"THE HERMIT."

59. Allegro poco Andante. *p* *pp* — Lambert.

"FREISCHÜTZ."

Weber.

60. Poco Andantino.

274
WALTZ: "FLOWER OF DAMASCUS."
Saverio.

"WALTZ FROM PURITANI."

Bellini.

276
PRAYER from "MOSES."
Rossini.

63.

"SIÉGE OF ROCHELLE."

277

Balfe.

"HAIL! STAR OF MARY."

Proch.

"THE TWO FRIENDS."

Polka Mazurka.
Laurent.

THE FOX HUNTERS.

LAST PART
CHARACTERISTIC STUDIES
FANTASIAS AND AIRS VARIES

LETZTER THEIL
CHARACTERISTISCHE STUDIEN
FANTASIEN UND VARIATIONEN

DERNIÈRE PARTIE
ÉTUDES CARACTÉRISTIQUES
FANTAISIES ET AIRS VARIES

LAST PART.

The following fourteen studies have been written with the special purpose of providing the student with suitable material with which to test his powers of endurance. In taking up these studies, the student will doubtless be fatigued, especially at the outset, by such of the numbers as require unusual length of breath. However, careful study and experience will teach him to triumph over such difficulties and will provide him with resources which, in turn, will enable him to master this particular phase of playing without difficulty. As a means to this end, I will point out the cantabile passages in particular, which should be played with the utmost expression, at the same time modifying the tone as much as possible. On the cornet, as with the voice, clear tones may be obtained by widening the lips, and veiled tones by contracting them. This circumstance affords the performer an opportunity to rest, while still continuing to play, and at the same time enables him to introduce effective contrasts into the execution. I repeat, that by little artifices of this kind, and by skillfully husbanding his resources, the player will reach the end of the longest and most fatiguing morceau, not only without difficulty, but even with a reserve of strength and power, which, when brought to bear on the final measures of a performance, never fails to produce its effect on an audience.

The twelve grand morceaux which follow are the embodiment of the various instructions contained in this volume; they will be found to contain all the articulations, all the difficulties, of which I have in turn already given the solution. They will also be found to contain melodies calculated to develop the taste of the student, and to render it as complete and as perfect as possible.

At this point my task as professor (employing as I now do the written instead of the spoken word) will end. There are things which appear clear enough when uttered *viva voce* but which cannot be committed to paper, without engendering confusion and obscurity, or without appearing puerile.

There are other things of so elevated and subtle a nature, that neither speech nor writing can clearly explain them. They are felt, they are conceived, but they are not to be explained, and yet these things constitute the elevated style, the grande école, which it is my ambition to institute for the cornet, even as they already exist for singing and the various kinds of instruments.

Those of my readers who are ambitious and who want to arrive at this exalted pitch of perfection, should, above all things, endeavor to hear good music well interpreted. They must seek out, amongst singers and instrumentalists, the most illustrious models, and this practice having purified their taste, developed their sentiments, and brought them as near as possible to the beautiful, may perhaps reveal to them the innate spark which may some day be destined to illumine their talent, and to render them worthy of being, in their turn, cited and imitated in the future.

LETZTER THEIL.

Ich habe die nachfolgenden vierzehn Etuden zu dem Zwecke componirt, den Schülern eine unbesiegbare Willenskraft einzuflössen. Es wird sie ohne allen Zweifel, besonders Anfangs, sehr ermüden, so langathmige Stücke zu blasen; Studium und Erfahrung werden sie jedoch lehren, über diese Schwierigkeiten zu triumphiren und die nöthigen Hülfsmittel zu finden, die sie ohne Hinderniss zum Ziel ihrer Aufgabe führen. Unter diesen Mitteln, welche fast ohne Ausnahme eine jede Composition darbietet, werde ich ihnen die Gesangspassagen bezeichnen, indem ich sie veranlasse, dieselben mit der höchsten Zartheit und im dunklen Klanggepräge zu blasen.—Man kann nämlich auf dem Cornet à Pistons ebenso, wie beim Gesange, helle Töne erhalten, indem man die Lippen öffnet und umschleierte Töne, indem man sie enger zusammenzieht.—Dies ist ein vortreffliches Mittel, um sich auszuruhen, ohne das Spiel zu unterbrechen und zugleich, um vortheilhafte Gegensätze in die Ausführung zu bringen. Ich wiederhole es, mit diesen kleinen Kunstgriffen wird der Virtuos, sobald er seine natürlichen Hilfsquellen mit Geschicklichkeit wahrnimmt, das längste und ermüdendste Musikstück zu Ende bringen, und zwar nicht nur ohne grosse Schwierigkeit sondern auch mit derjenigen Reserve von Kraft und Gewalt, die gerade in den letzten Takten eine unfehlbare Wirkung auf den Hörer ausüben.

Die zwölf grossen Stücke, welche darauf folgen, sind das Résumé der verschiedenen Anweisungen, welche dieses Werk enthält. Man findet in ihnen sämmtliche Articulationen, sämmtliche Passagen und Schwierigkeiten deren Lösung ich nach und nach im Vorhergehenden gegeben habe. Ausserdem findet man darin Melodien, die geeignet sind, den Geschmack des Schülers zu bilden und ihn so vollkommen und perfect als möglich zu machen.

Hier endet natürlich die Aufgabe des Lehrers, besonders dessen, der sich statt der mündlichen der schriftlichen Erklärung bedient. Es giebt Dinge, die man wohl mündlich auseinandersetzen kann, die aber eine schriftliche Erklärung nicht vertragen, ohne Verwirrung und Dunkelheit und ohne in Lächerlichkeit zu verfallen.

Es giebt aber wiederum andere Dinge, die so erhabener und subtiler Natur sind, dass sie sich überhaupt jeder mündlichen und schriftlichen Erklärung entziehen. Man kann sie nur fühlen, ahnen, nicht aber erklären. Diese Dinge machen den hohen Styl, die grosse Schule aus, die auch für das Cornet à Pistons zu gründen, ich den edlen Ehrgeiz besitze, wie sie bereits für den Gesang und die Mehrzahl der Instrumente bestehen.

Diejenigen Leser dieser Methode, welche jenen erhabenen Gipfel erreichen wollen, müssen sich vor allem bemühen, gute und gut ausgeführte Musik zu hören. Sie müssen sich unter den Sängern und Instrumentalisten eifrig die besten Vorbilder aufsuchen und dieser Verkehr wird, nachdem er ihren Geschmack gereinigt, ihr Gefühl erweckt und ihren Schönheitssinn möglichst entwickelt, vielleicht dereinst den Funken der Originalität entzünden, der dann ihr Talent erleuchtet und sie würdig macht, auch ihrerseits in der Zukunft als Muster angeführt und nachgeahmt zu werden.

DERNIÈRE PARTIE.

J'ai composé les quatorze études suivantes dans le but d'inculquer aux élèves une invincible force de volonté. Ils se fatigueront sans nul doute, surtout dans l'origine, en jouant des morceaux d'aussi longue haleine; l'étude, l'expérience leur apprendront à triompher de cette difficulté et à découvrir des ressources pour arriver sans encombre au bout de leur tâche. Parmi les moyens qu'offre presque invariablement toute composition, je leur signalerai les passages de chant, en les engageant à les rendre avec une extrême douceur en sombrant le son.—On peut, sur le cornet à pistons, obtenir, ainsi que le font les chanteurs, des sons clairs en ouvrant les lèvres, et des sons voilés en les resserrant.—Ce sera un excellent moyen de se reposer sans cesser de jouer, et en même temps d'introduire d'heureux contrastes dans l'exécution. Je le répète, avec ces petits artifices, ménageant ses resources avec adresse, le virtuose arrivera à la fin du morceau le plus long et le plus fatigant, non-seulement sans une grande difficulté, mais encore avec une réserve de force et de puissance dont l'effet dépensé aux dernières mesures est immanquable sur l'auditeur.

Les douze grands morceaux qui viennent ensuite sont le résumé des divers enseignements contenus dans ce volume: on y trouvera toutes les articulations, tous les traits, toutes les difficultés dont j'ai tour à tour donné précédemment la solution. On y trouvera, en outre, des mélodies propres à former le goût de l'élève, à le rendre aussi complet et aussi parfait que possible.

Là s'arrête naturellement ma tâche de professeur surtout de professeur employant l'écriture au lieu de la parole. Il y a des choses qui peuvent se transmettre de vive voix, mais qui ne sauraient être confiées au papier sans engendrer la confusion et l'obscurité, ou sans tomber dans l'enfantillage.

Il y a d'autres choses encore d'un ordre si élevé et si subtil qu'elles se refusent à l'interprétation de la parole aussi bien que de l'écriture. On les sent, on les devine, on ne les explique pas. Ces choses constituent le haut style, la grande École que j'ai la noble ambition de vouloir fonder pour le cornet à pistons, comme ils existent déjà pour le chant et pour la plupart des instruments.

Ceux des lecteurs de cette Méthode qui voudront atteindre à ces sommets élevés devront, avant tout, s'étudier à entendre de bonne musique bien interprétée. Parmi les chanteurs et les virtuoses instrumentistes, ils rechercheront assidûment les plus parfaits modèles, et ce commerce, après avoir épuré leur goût développé leur sentiment et les avoir conduits aussi près que possible de la perfection dans le beau, leur révélera peut-être l'étincelle originale qui doit un jour illuminer leur talent et les rendre dignes d'être à leur tour cités et imités dans l'avenir.

14 Characteristic STUDIES.
14 Characteristische STUDIEN.
14 ETUDES Caractéristiques.

1. Allegro moderato.

Fine.

rall.

D. C.

288

4. Allegro.

290

6. Moderato.

rall. a tempo

TWELVE

Celebrated Fantaisies and Airs Variés

by

ARBAN

CONTENTS

N⁰ 1. Fantaisie and Variations on a Cavatina from Beatrice di Tenda by Bellini 301
N⁰ 2. Fantaisie and Variations on "Actéon" 305
N⁰ 3. Fantaisie Brillante 309
N⁰ 4. Variations on a Tyrolean Song 313
N⁰ 5. Variations on a song "Vois-tu la neige qui brille" *The Beautiful Snow* . . 317
N⁰ 6. Cavatina and Variations 320
N⁰ 7. Air Varié on a Folk Song: "The Little Swiss Boy" 323
N⁰ 8. Caprice and Variations 327
N⁰ 9. Fantaisie and Variations on a German Theme 331
N⁰ 10. Variations on a favorite theme by C. M. von Weber 335
N⁰ 11. Fantaisie and Variations on "The Carnival of Venice" 339
N⁰ 12. Variations on a theme from "Norma" by V. Bellini 344

Cornet in B♭

Revised by Edwin Franko Goldman

N° I
Fantaisie and Variations
on a Cavatina
from Beatrice di Tenda by V. Bellini

J. B. Arban

Introduction
Andante

Cornet in B♭

Cornet in B♭

Var. III and Finale I

305

No. 2
Fantaisie and Variations
on
Acteon

Cornet in A

Revised by
Edwin Franko Goldman

J. B. Arban

Introduction
Andante

306

Cornet in A

Theme
Allegro

Cornet in A

Nº 3
Fantaisie Brillante

Cornet in B♭
Revised by Edwin Franko Goldman

J. B. Arban

Introd.
Allegro maestoso

Copyright MCMXII by Carl Fisher, New York.

310 Cornet in B♭

311

Cornet in B♭

No. 5
Variations
on a
Tyrolean Song

Cornet in B♭

Revised by
Edwin Franko Goldman

J. B. Arban

Cornet in B♭

315

316 Cornet in B♭

From + to + can be omitted

317

Cornet in B♭

Revised by
Edwin Franko Goldman

№ 9
Variations
on a song
Vois-tu la neige qui brille
(The Beautiful Snow)

J. B. Arban

Cornet in B♭

No. 10
Cavatina and Variations

Cornet in B♭
Revised by Edwin Franko Goldman
J. B. Arban

Cornet in B♭

Nº 6
Air Varié
on a Folk Song
The Little Swiss Boy

Revised by Edwin Franko Goldman

Cornet in B♭

J. B. Arban

Introd. Andante

325

Cornet in B♭

Cornet in B♭

Var IV et Finale
Allegro

Caprice and Variations

№ 7

Cornet in B♭
Revised by Edwin Franko Goldman
Andantino

J. B. Arban

Cornet in B♭

Revised by Edwin Franko Goldman

Nº 8
Fantaisie and Variations
on a German Theme

J. B. Arban

Allegro moderato

Theme
Andante

Cornet in B♭

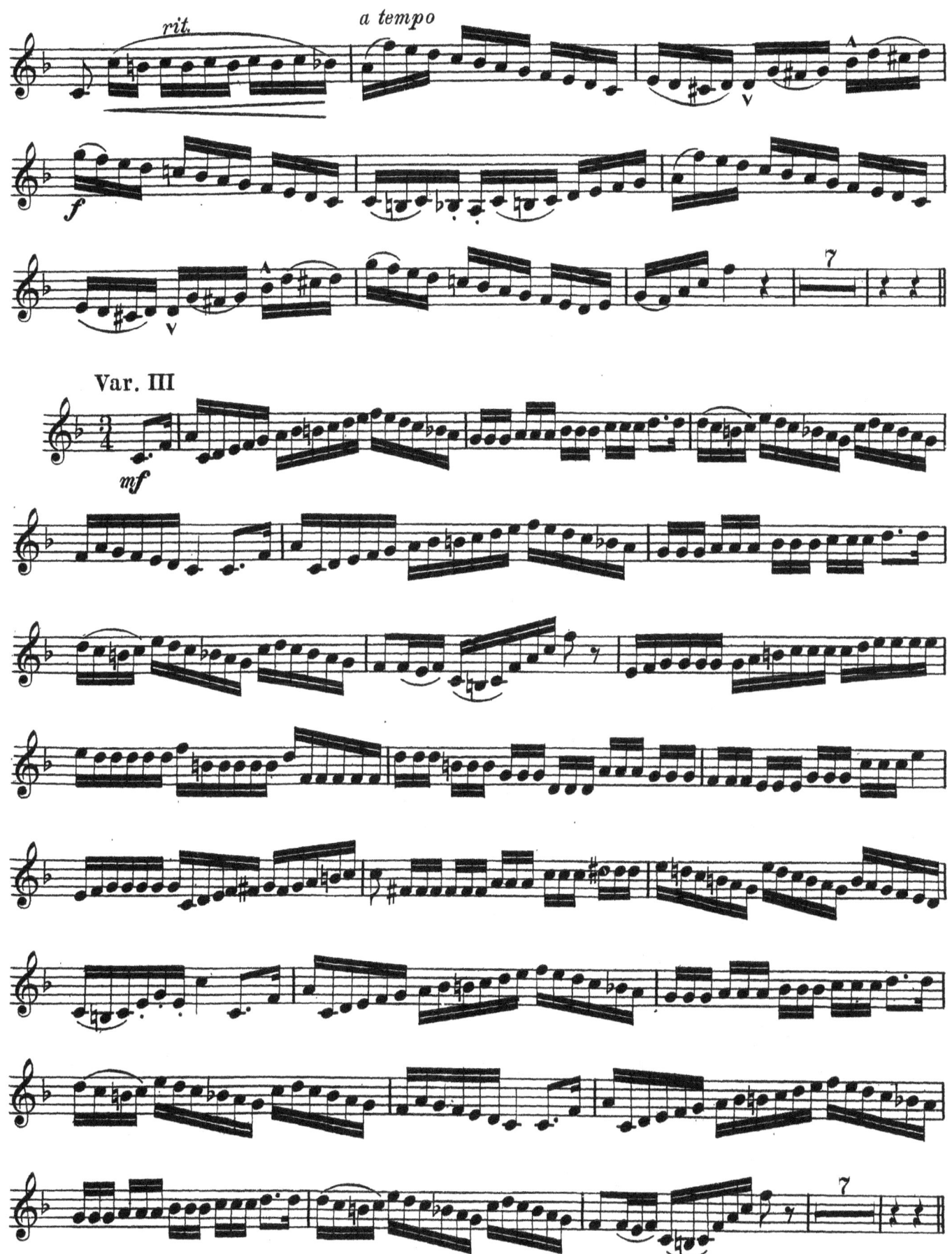

Cornet in B♭

Finale

No. 11
Variations
on a favorite theme
by
C. M. von Weber

Cornet in B♭

Revised by
Edwin Franko Goldman

J. B. Arban

Introd.
Allegro moderato

336

Cornet in B♭

Theme
Andante non troppo

Var. I

Var. II

Cornet in B♭

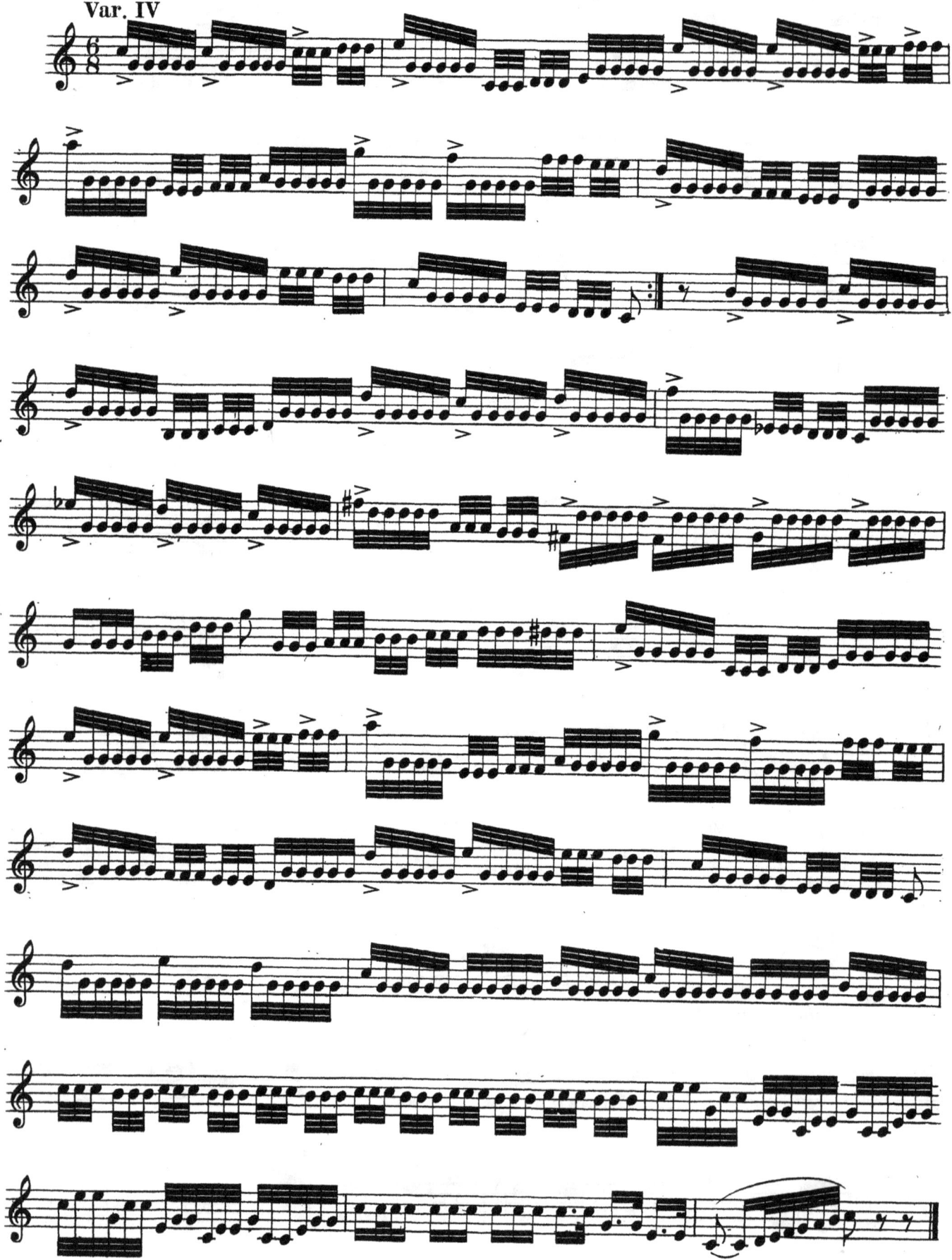

Nº 12
Fantaisie and Variations
on
The Carnival of Venice

Cornet in B♭
Revised by Edwin Franko Goldman

J. B. Arban

Introduction
Allegretto

Cornet in B♭

342

Cornet in B♭

Cornet in B♭

344

Cornet in B♭

Revised by
Edwin Franko Goldman

N.º 4
Variations
on a theme from
Norma
by V. Bellini

J. B. Arban

Cornet in B♭

346 Cornet in B♭

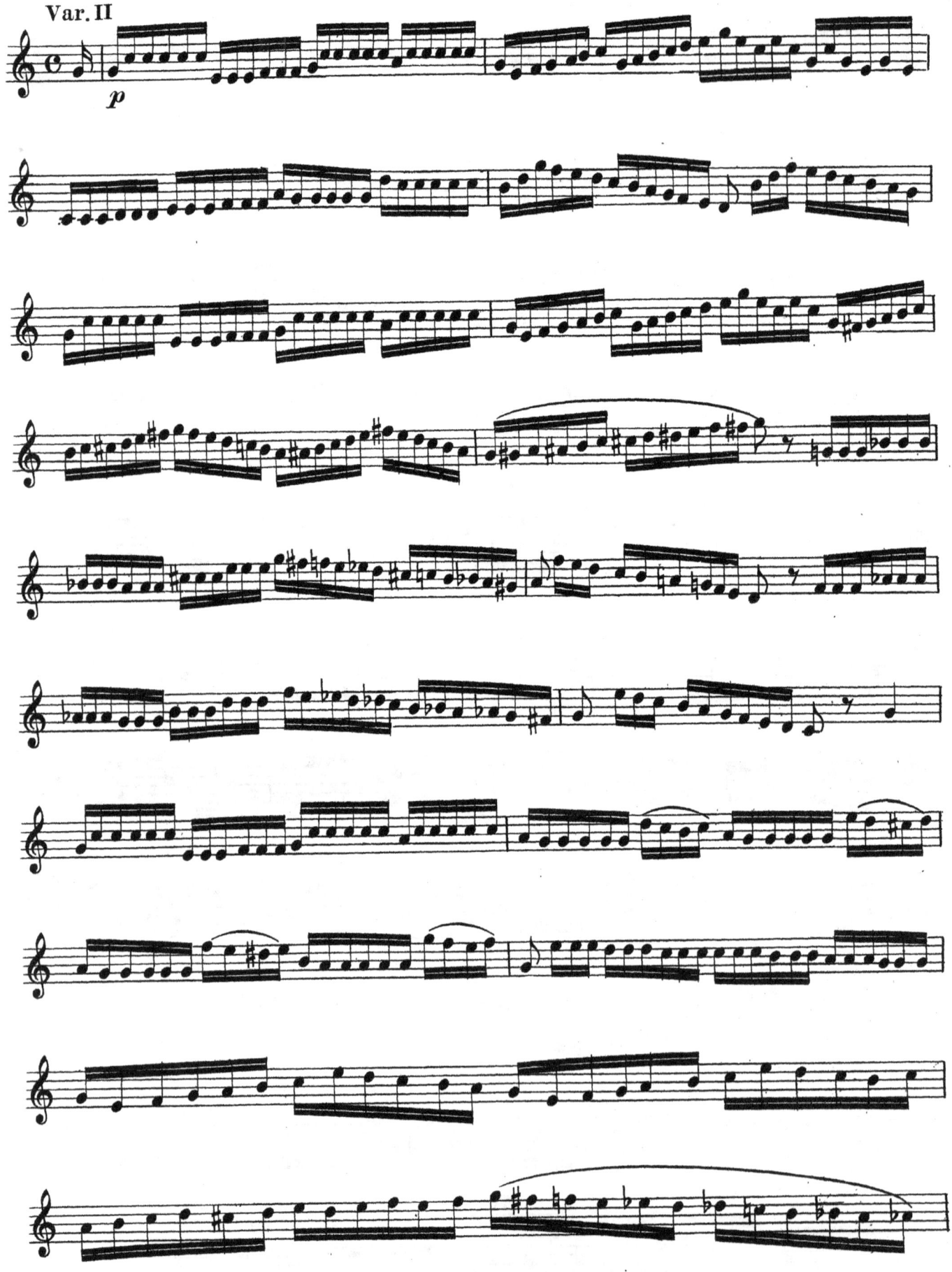

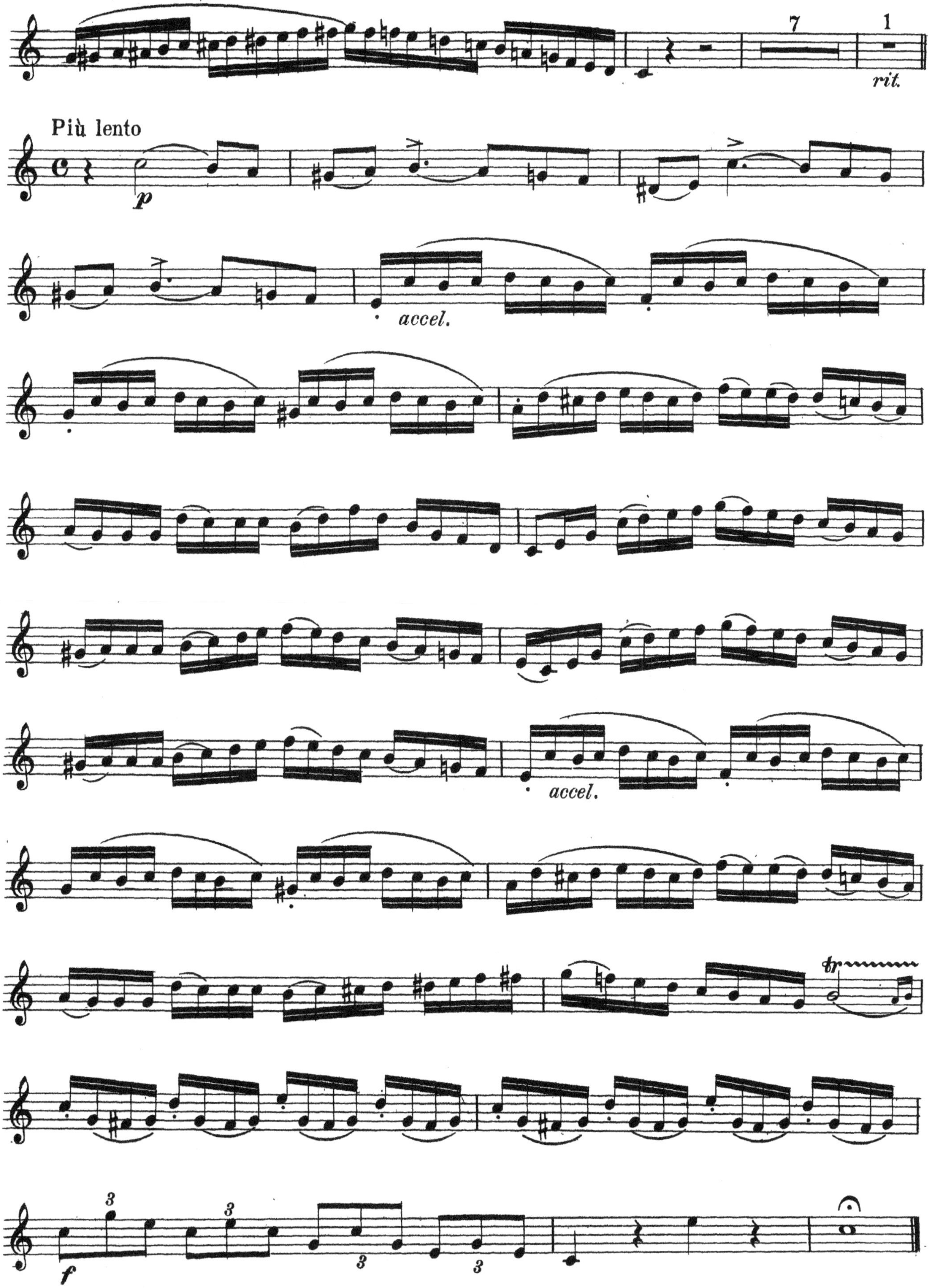
7
1
rit.
Più lento
p
accel.
accel.
tr
3
3
3
3
f

www.ingramcontent.com/pod-product-compliance
Lightning Source LLC
Chambersburg PA
CBHW081826170426
43202CB00019B/2966